GALILEE DIARY

Galilee Diary

*Reflections on
Daily Life in Israel*

MARC
ROSENSTEIN

URJ PRESS
New York, New York

Library of Congress Cataloging-in-Publication Data

Rosenstein, Marc, 1946–
    Galilee diary / Marc Rosenstein.—1st ed.
        p. cm.
    "The Galilee diary began as a weekly essay posted on the URJ website, created to serve
as a teaching aid to teachers in the Reform Movement."—Preface
    ISBN 978-0-8074-1078-3
    1. Israel—Social life and customs. 2. Israel—Politics and government. 3. Reform
Judaism—Israel. 4. Zionism and Judaism. 5. Galilee (Israel)—Description and travel.
6. Rosenstein, Marc, 1946– I. Title
    DS112.R747 2010
    956.9405′4—dc22
                            2009054383

"Introduction: Reflections on Reform Zionism" originally appeared,
in slightly different form, in *Reform Judaism*, Spring 2005.

For Tami

Contents

Preface

It is a commonplace that technology is making the world smaller—and hence, bringing Israel closer to the farthest reaches of the Diaspora. When I first visited Israel in 1962, air travel was a big deal. Many homes in Israel didn't have a telephone, and calling home to the United States was a major event, which I did only a couple of times during my six-month stay. I wrote aerogrammes that took ten days to get from Haifa to Chicago. Now we have webcams and e-mail, multiple daily nonstop flights, and kids on summer programs who talk to their parents in the United States several times a day on their cell phones, as they rappel down cliffs in the desert or wander the alleys of Meah Shearim.

And yet, the distance remains. Despite the media that stream information about Israel to the Diaspora, the opportunities for Jews to get a true sense of the landscape, the people, everyday life, culture, and human stories are few and far between. Filtered through the agendas of organized Jewish life or of sensationalist news media, diced and distorted into video montages and sound bites, what many Diaspora Jews see of Israel is a distressingly pale reflection of a rich and complex reality.

At the time of the outbreak of the Second Intifada, in 2000,

Rabbi Jan Katzew (then director of the Department of Lifelong Jewish Learning and now lead specialist at the Union for Reform Judaism) and I both found ourselves troubled by this frustrating sense of failed communication. We both felt that the entire relationship of North American Jews to Israel was being twisted and attenuated by a one-dimensional form of communication. So he invited me to begin an experiment, a web diary describing and reflecting on everyday life in Israel, emphasizing not the "blood and fire and pillars of smoke" that occupy the mainstream news media, but the small stories, the challenges and satisfactions, the frustrations and beauties encountered by the ordinary citizen living here.

Thus the Galilee Diary began, as a weekly essay posted on the URJ website, created to serve as a teaching aid to teachers in the Reform Movement. It turns out that the reality here in Israel must be rich indeed, for after 450 diary entries, I still have not run out of observations, experiences, and reflections to share with readers abroad. The experience of writing the diary has helped me see my own surroundings better, close as they are; and it seems, from occasional reader feedback and the increasing number of those who subscribe to the diary through the Ten Minutes of Torah program, that others have also found it helpful and interesting.

This book represents a collection of some of the highlights of the first eight years of the experiment. Together, the entries seek to provide a multidimensional look at Israel for the general reader as well as a resource for teachers and group leaders seeking materials that go behind the headlines. It is important to keep in mind that I am not a Middle East expert; my knowledge of Israeli politics and Israel's place in its geopolitical environment is that of an ordinary reader of newspapers. Therefore, almost none of the entries deal with the headlines themselves, or seek to explain or comment or predict. There are plenty of people far more qualified to undertake that task than I am, so I have not attempted to compete with them. I am, of course, not really an average Israeli, and my perspective and my choice of content reflect the fact that I am an immigrant from the United States, and a Reform Jewish educator—and that I live in the periphery. Life in the Galilee is no more or less authentic than life in Jerusalem, but it is different. I find these differences interesting and thought-provoking, and I hope to convey these unique experiences to the readers of *Galilee Diary*.

The characters that populate these entries are largely members of my family, or my neighbors in Shorashim. I didn't ask their permission to write about them, but tried to present them sympathetically. I hereby apologize if I have unintentionally misrepresented or offended anyone.

I have selected entries that seemed appropriate to me, edited and filled them out where necessary, and added some explanatory material. My son Joshua served as my first reader, editing, pointing out areas that needed clarification, and suggesting illustrations and explanations. This collaboration was fun for both of us, and Josh's sharp, critical eye contributed significantly to the clarity, consistency, and readability of the final product. Of course, I owe a debt of gratitude to Rabbi Jan Katzew, who was responsible for initiating *Galilee Diary* and for sustaining it all these years. I thank Rabbi Joan Farber for her encouragement and support (technical and moral), and the technical staff of the URJ who have kept *Galilee Diary* online and glitch-free for almost a decade. The editorial staff of the URJ Press did a lot of thoughtful and painstaking work on the book, and helped me rethink and rewrite and clarify many of the entries. Over the years, the *Diary* has drawn a stream of reader responses, both critical and complimentary. They have all been helpful and much appreciated; it is always nice to be reminded that there really is "somebody out there" reading and thinking about what I write.

No matter how successful I might be in bringing Israel to life for readers, their experience of Israel is still filtered through my interpretation; it is still, necessarily, secondhand. *Galilee Diary* can only really be seen as a success if it helps move its readers toward the decision to come and experience Israel directly. "Next year in Jerusalem"? Why not this year in the Galilee?

Introduction:

Reflections on Reform Zionism

Zionism burst onto the scene of Jewish history more than a century ago, the result of the meeting of three powerful forces: traditional Jewish messianic hope, secular humanism, and modern nationalism. Suddenly, the longstanding acceptance of the Jews as a people whose land existed only in memory and in hope gave way to the feeling that we could, by our own actions, build a Jewish state in our ancestral homeland—and that in so doing we would become a "normal" people, with a culture rooted in a place.

From its inception, everyone understood what Zionism was—and yet, at the same time, its exact definition was always unclear. A Jewish state? Of course! But just what kind of Jewish state? What vision, exactly, were we trying to realize? From the beginning, Zionism was hyphenated: practical, political, cultural, religious, secular, socialist, liberal, revisionist. Now we can add Reform, Conservative, Messianic/settler; the list goes on and on.

I am, and have always been, a Reform Zionist. My father came from a traditional home; my mother's father was a socialist. Both were Zionists who toyed with the idea of *aliyah* in the mid-1940s, and they brought Zionism to their involvement in Reform synagogues. So for me, the synthesis was natural, taken for granted. My parents, and Rabbi Robert Samuels, then assistant rabbi at North Shore Congregation Israel in Glencoe, Illinois, encouraged me to participate in the Eisendrath Israel Exchange Program. That real-life, intensive experience of Israel confirmed my Zionism—and my feeling that out of all the different styles of Zionism I could embrace, I was definitely a Reform Zionist. I felt Israel had to be the messianic state—not in the apocalyptic sense but in the utopian sense, that the whole exercise would be pointless, or worse, if it were not driven by a vision of Israel as the embodiment of Jewish values in a real state, in the real world, in real time.

Ever since that time, I have struggled to define how the implications of this understanding of Reform Zionism would affect the rest of my own life. After years of working in Jewish education in the United States, interspersed with periods of working and studying in Israel, I finally concluded that my personal variety of Reform Zionism required me to make my home in Israel and to contribute to the building of the Zionist utopia with my own hands. My decision was more emotional and cultural than ideological. My wife and I both love the Hebrew language and Israeli culture. We love the landscapes of Israel, the Galilee in particular. And I remain here not because I have to and not because I felt out of place in the United States (in fact, the Lincoln Memorial remains a site of pilgrimage for me), but because I feel that being here is the fulfillment of what it means to be a Reform Jew.

I see Israel as the proving ground for Jewish values. We have to face the question of how we live out Jewish values when we have sovereignty, independence, and power. This huge challenge—of translating Jewish values into a society and into a state worthy of being called Jewish—is invigorating, but it is also very difficult, not nearly as simple as it sounded when we were standing at Mt. Sinai, saying, "We will do and we will listen," before we had any idea of what it is like to run a government, serve a diverse population, deal with poverty, and make war and peace.

The community where I live is a prime example of the dilemmas involved in creating a state that is both Jewish and democratic. In 1990, my family made *aliyah* to Shorashim, a small moshav in the central Galilee, founded ten years earlier by a group of young North American immigrants. When we arrived, the community consisted of thirty families, had a socialist economic structure, and functioned as a liberal religious congregation (affiliated with the Masorti [Conservative] movement). We felt like we had arrived in a utopia, not only because we found the communal religious life and the mutual economic responsibility a perfect fit for our ideals, but also because it turned out that the community was active in promoting Arab-Jewish cooperation through a joint day camp and other activities (about 80 percent of the citizens of the rural Galilee are Arabs; the children are third-generation Israelis). We so treasured this community and its values that my wife Tami and I immediately took on active roles in important committees: recruitment and strategic planning. We had scarcely finished unpacking when the strategic planning committee found itself presiding over a difficult two-year process of privatization, as the majority of the members had come to feel that the value of individual economic autonomy was more important to them than the value of communal mutual responsibility So, just as in the state as a whole, socialism gave way to private enterprise. We reluctantly gave up on one ideal in favor of another: the solidarity of the community and its democratic right to choose its own path.

On the recruitment committee, we were strong advocates for screening applicants for membership, to ensure that new families were committed to an active community based on a liberal approach to Jewish observance. We were worried that by accepting just anyone we would run the risk of losing the special Shabbat atmosphere, the joyous extended-family-like holiday observances, and the strong sense of shared values and shared experiences. But as the years went by, we began to question our own position. On the one hand, we felt we had a right to maintain and preserve our community; on the other hand, we suffered a nagging moral doubt about living in a community whose admission criterion is not just "Jews only," but "Jews *like us* only." Given my liberal beliefs, it is pretty hard to look my middle-class, professional, Muslim Arab friend and colleague in the eye and say, "Sorry, you can't buy a house here." And yet, if she does buy a house here, that's one less person I can call on for a *shivah minyan,* one less person who will share the load of reading Torah and providing *Kiddush.* In Shorashim, as in the State of Israel at large, it's hard to know where to draw the line between collective self-interest and universal values.

And so I find myself, like the State of Israel, subject to two powerful currents that often seem to pull in opposite directions simultaneously. On the one hand, there is my ethnic, national identity as a Jew, nourished by language, holidays, and collective memory; by a powerful sense of rootedness in the historical land; by the joy, finally, of empowerment after centuries of powerlessness. On the other hand, there is my Jewish commitment to justice and mercy, to knowing the heart of the stranger, to being a holy people, to living by the words of the prophets, to *tikkun olam* (repairing the world). Living here as a Reform Zionist means constantly struggling to maintain the balance. It's like a high-wire act—difficult and scary and dangerous, requiring years of intricate training and preparation, but unbelievably exhilarating when you finally get it right.

In our synagogue, in Shorashim, we recite at Shabbat morning services the official prayer of the chief rabbinate for the State of Israel, which says, in part, that the state is "the first flowering of our redemption." I think that the author of the prayer meant this as a fact. For me it is a prayer—what we are striving to achieve—but it will take more than prayer to make it happen.

The work to make it happen is what I'm trying to do here as a Reform Zionist.

PART I

Reflections
on Zionism

1. Homelessness *(February 3, 2008)*

So the Lord God banished him from the Garden of Eden, to till the soil from which he was taken. He drove the man out, and stationed east of the Garden of Eden the cherubim and the fiery ever-turning sword, to guard the way to the tree of life.

—Genesis 3:22–23

In the annual cycle of the Torah reading, by mid-February we have finished with the Genesis narratives, gotten into and out of Egypt, and received the Torah. From now until Simchat Torah, we'll be in the desert, blowing our chance, because of our faithlessness, for a quick journey to our new-old homeland. Eight months of Torah readings, covering forty years of history, about the wandering Jews. You might think that the Torah, being the basic, formative document of our collective life, would have taken place in our homeland—and yet, ironically, after a few generations of the Patriarchs' and Matriarchs' comings and goings in the region, we spend the next four books imagining the land, looking forward or backward to it—but not living in it. Indeed, I find it fascinating how central the theme of exile is throughout the Bible:

- Adam and Eve are banished from the Garden of Eden (Genesis 3:23)
- God punishes Cain by forcing him to wander, away from his homeland, for the rest of his life (Genesis 4:12–13)
- Abraham leaves home (Genesis 12:1) and then leaves his new home (Genesis 12:11)
- Abraham and Sarah drive Hagar and Ishmael away from their home (Genesis 21:9–20)
- Lot and his family struggle against the decree to leave their home in Sodom (Genesis 19)
- Rebekah sends Jacob off to Haran after the deception regarding Esau's blessing (Genesis 27:41–45); and he leaves again to go down to Egypt
- Joseph is carried into Egyptian exile against his will, but rapidly "makes it" there, assimilating so successfully that his brothers fail to recognize him (Genesis 37–50)

And the list goes on: Where is Moses' home, exactly? The crisis of the spies and the sentence of forty years' wandering. David—and Elijah—on the lam. The prophets' threats of exile—and the real exile to Babylonia in 586 B.C.E. Jeremiah. Ezekiel. Esther and the vulnerability of the exiles. Ezra and Nehemiah and the exiles' reluctance to return.

Homelessness seems to be a powerful motif running through the Bible. It is the ultimate threat, the ultimate punishment—and, at the same time, a common experience. The Bible seems fascinated with the situation of being homeless, uprooted, without a place. Perhaps being homeless is so threatening because it means being powerless. The exile is always vulnerable, always dependent, can never unpack. Moreover, I think, place to a large extent defines our identity. If we have no place that is stable, if we have no address—then who are we? And yet, at the same time, being an exile makes you light on your feet. Never unpacking means you can be driven by your values, not just by the price of real estate. Not being committed to a patch of earth means you can be committed fully to God and God's demands. Roots sustain you—but they also hold you down. To put the matter in a contemporary perspective, having a state is a great blessing—and a great burden of responsibility.

Isaac never leaves home. Moses never gets there. Between these two poles of experience live most of the leading characters of the Bible—and most of us: constantly seeking the balance between space and place, between being settled and being unsettled, between the need to be rooted and the need to move on, between the known— solid, secure, comfortable—and the as yet unknown—challenging, scary, yet full of promise.

2. Staying Put *(December 2, 2001)*

The Eternal One said to Abram, "Go forth from your land, your birthplace, your father's house, to the land that I will show you."

—Genesis 12:1

My family made *aliyah* on the day after Saddam Hussein invaded Kuwait, so our absorption year was the year of the First Gulf War (1991), during which the five of us endured Scud attacks in our sealed room, wearing gas masks, together with the dog, the cat, and a hamster (who didn't have gas masks). Although it turned out, in the end, that none of the Iraqi missiles ever carried a chemical warhead, the country mobilized for a chemical attack, and the fear generated thereby sometimes bordered on hysteria. It was a time when many Israelis and many Jews spending the year here on educational programs left the country. And people said to us, "You sure picked a good time to make *aliyah*!" I'm not sure why it never entered our minds to leave. We don't see ourselves as brave, we were not unhappy living in the

United States before we came here, we are not driven to be here out of a sense of religious commandedness, we are not so essential to the security of the state. Inertia. Adventure. A tendency to try to calculate risks rationally, not emotionally. Fatalism. Optimism. Unwillingness to admit a mistake. All of the above. In any case, it seemed the natural thing to do to simply go on with our routine and take the risk and fear and discomfort as an adventure.

When people say, "You sure picked a good time to make *aliyah*!" we have always responded, "Yeah, so when was there ever a good time to make *aliyah*?" Go to the microfilm drawers and pick a newspaper from any day in the past century. Try to find a good day for making *aliyah*. . . .

In the past year, a number of our friends and acquaintances, and by no means only recent arrivals, have decided to take a "leave of absence" from Israel for a few years (at least). It has not been a good year for optimists, and it has gotten almost impossible to find one. The screaming, bloody headlines attack you on one side, while the dull pounding of doubt about the morality of our collective behavior hounds you on the other side. You really don't see a way out, or what you can do to make a difference, or any leader worthy of following. You see the crowds of your fellow Jews and fellow Israelis chanting "Death to the Arabs" at soccer games and you wonder who made up the slogan "We are one." You are tongue-tied when your kid asks your advice about signing on for an extra year in the army, to be an officer. And to top it off, you see yourself fulfilling the old joke about how to make a small fortune in Israel (by coming with a large one).

You actually find yourself wondering whether this whole enterprise is right—and if it is, whether it is realistic. You remember how many times, in discussions of Jewish history, the question is asked, "How could they not have seen the handwriting on the wall?"

And yet, for us (and for most other Israelis, immigrants and sabras alike), the response to all of this is not a flight out of Ben Gurion Airport. We complain and shake our heads, we share black humor, we turn off the news—and we go on with the routines of work and recreation, family and friends. The gas mask is in the closet. The kid hides his rifle under the bed on Shabbat. We open our bags automatically for inspection whenever we enter the mall. We know better than to believe in Bush, Sharon, Peres, and Arafat.

We make nasty comments about the lady who cuts in line in the bank and the guy who passes in the no-passing zone. We smile when it rains and delight in the rainbow across the valley and the wildflowers sprouting among the litter. And we are sad to be so far from our extended family.

We know that we don't know what will happen tomorrow, and while that is stressful, it is also exciting. Maybe that's the secret of sticking it out here: being able to enjoy free-falling, knowing but not knowing that the parachute will open just in time. Consciousness? Faith? A personality disorder? Historical obligation or personal need or divine commandment?

Can't say. But in spite of everything, here we are.

3. Crossing the Border *(January 11, 2004)*

Last week I flew from Toronto to New York, and when I handed my passport and customs form to the immigration officer, a big beefy guy with a blond crew cut, he asked, "I see you're an American citizen. Why do you live in Israel?" My jaw dropped. I couldn't even begin to answer, and was moved to smile as I contemplated the impossibility of explaining to him what I can hardly explain to myself—and briefly, yet. My smile did not cut it, and while I was searching for something to say, he continued, "You don't like it in the United States?" "No, that's not it. I do like the United States, it's just . . ." By then he had stamped my passport and handed it back to me without expression. What was he thinking? Does he ask this often? What answers does he get?

I guess I could have quoted him this midrash, from *Sifrei D'varim* (a collection of interpretations of the books of Numbers and Deuteronomy, from about 500 C.E.), *R'eih*:

> It happened that Rabbi Judah ben Baterah and Rabbi
> Matyah ben Charash and Rabbi Chaninah ben Achi and
> Rabbi Joshua ben Yonatan were traveling abroad. . . . When
> they remembered the Land of Israel, they lifted up their
> eyes and their tears flowed, and they tore their clothes, and
> read this verse: ". . . When you have occupied [the land] and
> settled in it, take care to observe all the laws and rules that I
> have set before you this day" [Deuteronomy 11:31–32]. And
> they returned home, and said: "Dwelling in the Land of
> Israel outweighs all of the commandments in the Torah."

Why do I live in Israel? Because no matter how emancipated we are in Chicago, no matter how rich a Jewish life we live in Toronto, no matter what wonderful traditions of social involvement we maintain in the North American Diaspora, it is still the *next best thing* to being *there*—there in the Promised Land, there in the only place where *all* the laws and rules are relevant. Note that the four Rabbis in the midrash did not weep because they had been exiled, because they were persecuted or rootless. They were only on a business trip or maybe even a vacation cruise. They wept when they realized how much of the Torah they were setting aside by absenting themselves from *Eretz Yisrael*. In voluntarily leaving the land, even temporarily, they were abandoning dozens of "mitzvah opportunities."

Of course, the first thing that comes to mind when we think of "land-dependent mitzvot" is the whole complex of laws surrounding the Temple cult. However, even in the absence of the Temple and sacrifices, there are many mitzvot that are only relevant within the borders of Eretz Yisrael, such as tithing and the Sabbatical year. Traditionally, that's the understanding of what the Rabbis were crying over.

However, I would like to suggest another way to understand the

Rabbis' tears. We have in our tradition the concepts of *kiddush HaShem* and *chilul HaShem,* the sanctification and profanation of God's name, respectively. If Jews do something morally heroic, they bring honor to Judaism and the Jewish people and proclaim the sanctity of God's name (*kiddush HaShem*); if Jews behave in a particularly nasty way in the world, they besmirch the Jewish people, the Jewish religion, and God's name (*chilul HaShem*). It seems to me that a Jewish state magnifies the significance of these concepts: The behavior of the state in the world reflects, willy-nilly, on Judaism. And if I live in a Jewish state, as a citizen in a democracy, I take on responsibility for this reflection. The state's actions are my actions. I am not judged just for my individual actions, but for the actions of the state that represents me. The renewal of Jewish life in Israel has opened anew many mitzvah opportunities — but it has by the same token laid upon us new responsibilities. Mitzvot are, after all, not good deeds but commandments. So if Jews are commanded to act justly in economic matters, a Jewish state must be committed as a state to social justice. The state moves Jewish values from the personal realm to the national, where they are a lot more complicated to implement. It's a daunting responsibility — but according to the Torah we were promised this land so we could implement the Torah's vision of a good society in a sovereign state.

For two thousand years the Jewish people wept at being unable to keep all the laws of the Torah, for we had neither the Holy Land nor state sovereignty. Now we have both, and the enormity of the responsibility is enough to make you cry! But that's why we're here, and there's something exhiliarating about the challenge. Now how could I have explained that to the immigration officer?

4. Justice, Justice *(February 1, 2004)*

Our staff at the Galilee Foundation for Value Education has been asked to plan a field day on social justice for the tenth grade at our regional public high school. We'll be dividing them into groups, each of which will explore a different issue for the day. One will deal with the topic of labor relations. There is, of course some irony in the fact that as of this writing there's a good probability that the whole activity will be canceled because of an expected wave of strikes by teachers and maintenance workers. In any case, labor relations is a particularly interesting topic in Israel, as the founders of the state were socialists; we had labor unions here long before we had a state, and for generations the state bureaucracy and the union bureaucracy were intertwined (pathologically so, it seems in retrospect). But that's not all. One of the dominant themes of Zionism from the beginning—and not only socialist Zionism—was the centrality of physical labor in the revitalization of the Jewish people. In returning to our land, we were being reborn normal, healthy, rooted, and self-sufficient. No more the stereotype of the *luftmensch* (one who lives on air)! Jewish mothers would be proud to raise not doctors and accountants, but farmers and mechanics.

One of the most remarkable figures in Zionist history was A. D. Gordon, who at the age of forty-seven (in 1903) left his white-collar existence in Russia and immigrated to Palestine, where he worked for the rest of his life (almost twenty years) as an agricultural laborer. Charismatic and articulate, he became a kind of guru to a whole generation—and his writings are still studied. For example:

> We ourselves must do all the work, from the least stren-
> uous, cleanest, and most sophisticated, to the dirtiest
> and most difficult. In our own way, we must feel what a
> worker feels and think what a worker thinks—then, and
> only then, shall we have a culture of our own, for then we
> shall have a life of our own. . . . Only by making Labor,
> for its own sake, our national ideal shall we be able to
> cure ourselves of the plague that has affected us for many

generations and mend the rent between ourselves and Nature. . . . We must all work with our own hands.

This mind-set gave rise to the ideal — and policy — of *avodah ivrit:* Zionist settlers should not hire Arab laborers to do their dirty work, but instead, should employ the newly created Jewish peasants and laborers. This ideal, of course, turned out to be a double-edged sword; the drive to *productivizatzia* ("productivization") and self-sufficiency also drove the local Arabs out of the economy and created deep-seated resentments, the consequences of which Israelis are still suffering.

As the twentieth century wore on, the proletarian vision of bourgeois, college-educated idealists dreaming of romantically dirty fingernails collided with the bourgeois vision of thousands of poor refugees from Europe and North Africa dreaming of a nice house in the suburbs and a comfortable, middle-class life.

Therefore, in order to teach our students about labor relations we will take them to visit factories turning out garments for major international brands, where all the sewing machines are operated by young Arab women working at minimum wage, and then we will visit prosperous Galilean fruit orchards, all of whose workers send their pay home to Thailand. If we should run into the spirit of A. D. Gordon, with his long white beard and his hoe, how will we even begin to explain ourselves?

5. Zionism, Straight Up *(February 15, 2004)*

Several years ago, after intensive negotiations, the government set up a program whereby candidates for conversion to Judaism may attend a pluralistic preparatory course, taught by representatives of the different movements, prior to undergoing a test and ceremony that conforms to Orthodox standards. For the past few months I have been teaching one of these courses for new immigrant soldiers.

The course is offered as part of basic training and, until the current round of budget cuts, was even available to soldiers who are Jewish already according to halachah, but who want to learn more about their roots.

The kids in my classes, about two-thirds of them girls, are graduates of *Na'aleh,* (an acronym for "Youth Making Aliyah before Their Parents," but also a word meaning "We will go up"—or "We will immigrate"), a Jewish Agency program in which teenagers from certain communities (mainly the former Soviet Union but also Eastern Europe and Latin America) make *aliyah* in tenth grade and attend boarding school, in the hope that their families will follow them once they are established here. Many of them are halachically Jewish, but many are not. By the time they get to the army, they have completed an Israeli high school education, and so have gotten a fairly strong dose of Israeli acculturation. This does not mean, however, that they know anything about Judaism.

Conditions at the base are good by army standards, but not exactly conducive to serious learning. They are doing this course— eight periods a day of classes—while also going through basic training; thus, they often arrive in class after a night of three hours' sleep, or leave in the middle to do guard duty, and so on. But these are kids who left home at the age of fifteen, voluntarily, to embark on an adventure in Israel. Some did it out of Jewish commitment, some out of a passionate sense of Zionism, some simply seeking a challenge or a change. They don't have to be here, and they don't have to be serving in the army or studying Judaism. So they stand up during class if they feel they are falling asleep. And they ask a lot of questions—and think about the answers— and write them down.

This weekend Tami and I went along with them on a Shabbat retreat at a modern Orthodox seminar center in the Golan Heights. Their officers—girls a year or two older than they are—are impressive role models for them: bright, thoughtful, open-minded, and deeply committed to their task and to their soldiers. Despite stormy weather, we had a lovely Shabbat. There were lots of special moments. One for me was seeing A., a tall blond who looks just like the son of a Ukrainian army officer (which he is), dancing at the front of the line during the *Kabbalat Shabbat* service, his rifle banging against the backs of his legs (in basic training you are never allowed to part with your weapon, ever!). Another was when the commander of the program gave a little sermon after dinner, and ended with *"Shabbat shalom!"* They responded in one voice, loud and clear: *"Shabbat shalom,* program commander, sir!"

Perhaps the most moving—and interesting and strange—experience during that Shabbat was hearing which song on their song-sheets they sang most eagerly (and frequently): a catchy pop tune by the popular songwriter Uzi Chitman (1952–2004), the chorus of which goes like this:

> Here I was born
> Here my children were born
> Here I built my home with my own two hands
> Here you are also with me, and
> Here also a thousand friends
> And after two thousand years—the end of my
> wanderings

In their joyful singing of a song I never took seriously before, they reminded me, in case I had forgotten, just what Zionism is.

6. Solidarity *(February 27, 2005)*

Thus said the Lord of Hosts, the God of Israel, to the whole community, which I exiled from Jerusalem to Babylon: Build houses and live in them, plant gardens and eat their fruit. Take

wives and beget sons and daughters; and take wives for your
sons and give your daughters to husbands, that they may bear
sons and daughters. Multiply there, do not decrease. And
seek the welfare of the city to which I have exiled you and
pray to the Lord in its behalf; for in its prosperity you shall
prosper. . . .

For thus said the Lord: When Babylon's seventy years are
over, I will take note of you, and I will fulfill to you My promise of favor—to bring you back to this place.

—Jeremiah 29:4–7, 10

Prior to the destruction of the First Temple (586 B.C.E.), Jeremiah
prophesied against rebelling against Babylonia. His message was
ignored: The people believed that God would support their struggle
and prevent the destruction of the Temple and Jewish sovereignty.
When the disaster occurred, he preached words of comfort, advising
the people to accept their fate and await God's restoration of their
sovereignty. And indeed, not seventy years later, but already in 538
B.C.E., the Persians conquered Babylonia and offered the exiled Jews
the opportunity to return to their land and rebuild their Temple.
They did not, however, offer the Jews political independence.

I wonder if Jeremiah realized what he was getting into with this
prophecy. God instructed the Israelites to make themselves at home
in Babylonia: to build houses, to raise grandchildren, to pray for
the prosperity of their new home. And to be ready, bags packed,
to return in seventy years! Sure enough, the Persians conquered
the Babylonians and allowed the Israelites to return—but by then,
they had taken out mortgages, enrolled the grandchildren in school,
opened thriving businesses, learned the language and the culture
of their exilic home—they had unpacked their bags. Needless to
say, there was no mass return. They became part of the exile and it
became part of them, and so it has been ever since. Individual Jews
seeking personal fulfillment and small groups fleeing the collapse of
their collective exilic home have made their way to Israel over the

years, but the majority of the Jews of the world keep their suitcases out of sight and out of mind, in the attic.

Ever since the Babylonian exile, there has been tension between the claim of the Jews who stayed in or returned to Israel to be the center, the authority, the bearers of authentic Judaism, and the claim of the leaders of Diaspora Jewish communities—who have often surpassed the Jews of Israel in scholarship, cultural creativity, and numbers— that dominance should be determined by quality, not merely by location. This was true in the Talmudic period, and in the Middle Ages, and it continues in our time. Many of us Israelis perceive ourselves as the true, authentic bearers of the fate of the Jewish people, putting our lives on the line to reassert our place in history and geography and to restore our ancient glory, while Diaspora Jews have missed the boat, choosing to enjoy the fleshpots of Babylonia/Miami/Berlin (ha!) as they blindly await their disappearance by assimilation or anti-Semitic violence. Thus, we Israelis have a right to the financial and political support of Diaspora Jews, whether they provide it out of guilt for staying safely far away, or out of a vicarious need to "be with us," drawing pride and a strengthened identity through their connection with us. This sense of entitlement to the support of world Jewry led to an Israeli outcry a year ago, when American Jewish fund-raisers tried to campaign for contributions to help the large numbers of Israelis living in poverty. We resented being presented as "charity cases," as no different from the helpless paupers of the Pale of Settlement from whom we have worked so hard to distance ourselves. We expect Diaspora support not as poor Jews, but as builders of the Jewish state, as bearers of Jewish national destiny.

For years, this asymmetry grated on the sensibilities of many (but not all) Diaspora Jews, who resented being seen as somehow inauthentic Jews, valuable only inasmuch as they could be exploited. While for many of us nothing has changed, it seems to me that in the past decade we are seeing a shift away from the classical Zionist view that the Diaspora is an aberration destined to disappear, toward a sense of symmetry and partnership. More and more Israelis are discovering that there is more than one way to Jewish authenticity—that the institutions built and supported by Jews in the Diaspora are worthy not of disdain, but of imitation; and that the huge expenditures of resources, energies, and creativity by Diaspora Jews on Jewish life in their own communities should command respect and admiration.

It may well be that We Are One, but we are learning that it is OK for us to be different from each other—and that Oneness should imply *mutual* respect.

7. The View from Here *(July 30, 2006)*

> As I see them from the mountaintops,
> Gaze on them from the heights,
> There is a people that dwells apart,
> Not reckoned among the nations,
> Who can count the dust of Jacob,
> Number the dust-cloud of Israel?
> May I die the death of the upright,
> May my fate be like theirs!
> —Numbers 23:9–10 (Balaam's attempt to curse Israel)

It has been heartwarming over the past several weeks to experience the great outpouring of support from world Jewry for Israel in its struggle against Hezbollah. A flood of personal e-mails and phone calls to me and my northern neighbors, countless forwards of essays expounding upon the justice of Israel's cause and exposing the bias and anti-Semitism and hypocrisy of the media, offers of help, solidarity campaigns and rallies, and emergency fund drives. The Jewish world knows how to mobilize in an emergency, and there is nothing like an old-fashioned war, with good guys and bad guys, to get us to put aside our divisions and differences and mobilize to save Jews in distress. This war has had the same effect inside Israel, calling forth massive efforts to send snacks and socks to the soldiers at the front, invitations to northerners to come stay in the south, and volunteer heroes to help deliver food to shut-ins and entertain children in bomb shelters. If American synagogues are putting up banners of support, here large companies are sponsoring patriotic billboards along the highways ("We will win!").

The fact that this war came upon us so suddenly, or so it seemed, without a buildup, based on a sudden provocation out of the blue and a lightning Israeli response, helped create this impressive unity of support. No one had time to think about it, to deliberate on what we should do, to prepare. It was just, Boom!, and there we were, willy-nilly, dragged into a war by an incomprehensibly cruel enemy against whom the natural and automatic reaction is to strike hard and fast, since our adversary doesn't understand reason, only force. What was there to debate?

Just like the response of Americans to 9/11—Israelis' first response to this war was to feel an absolute sense of being unjustly and unfairly attacked for no rational reason. We were clearly victims of evil.

Of course, it turns out, just as with any war—and even in the responses to 9/11—there are things to debate, and the questioning voices are already being heard from various points on the political spectrum. Were we properly prepared for the obvious? Should we have acted sooner? Was the massive bombing of Lebanon a wise course of action? Were there agreed-upon goals to the war? Are we being exploited by the United States? Could we have prevented this by a different policy toward Syria? Toward Iran? Toward Lebanon?

Israel's unofficial motto for at least sixty years has been "*Ein breira*—We have no choice." It explains why we have a universal draft, why we have nuclear weapons, why we drained the swamps and absorbed the immigrants. It is a powerful slogan, as it implies that we bear no responsibility for our actions, and are forced to act by circumstances or in response to others' actions. We are powerless to act differently. As Golda famously said, "We can forgive the Arabs for killing our sons, but not for making our sons into killers." This slogan implies that whatever we do is morally justified: They made us do it—what else could we do?

For American Jews, this view of history means that they can identify unreservedly with Israel and support it with no holds barred, and even use the emergency to galvanize and unite and revitalize their own community. For Israel is, once again, the victim of the eternal effort to wipe out the Jews.

Alas, for us Israelis it means that when the dust settles, there will most likely be bitter recriminations, political upheaval, and commissions of inquiry. For the fact is that with the creation of a Jewish state—what the great historian of the Holocaust, Professor Judah Bauer, has called "the Jewish emergence from powerlessness"—we, its citizens, do indeed always have a choice, and we have to live with the consequences of the choices we make. There is a contradiction between the refrain that "We have no choice" and the belief that Israel is now a sovereign, powerful state responsible for its actions. We cannot have it both ways. It is comfortable to see ourselves as powerless victims of a cruel world, but that view undermines the Zionist vision of Jewish sovereignty and seems to me an evasion of responsibility for the very real power we do wield in the world.

8. Remembering and Forgetting *(December 31, 2006)*

> If I forget you, O Jerusalem, let my right hand wither, let my tongue stick to my palate if I cease to think of you . . .
> —Psalm 137:5

Abraham has no sooner arrived in Israel the first time, obeying God's command to uproot himself and settle here, when he leaves for Egypt to escape a famine. Later, he sends back to the old country for a wife for his son. Isaac and Rebekah too send their son away to seek a wife—and he stays abroad for decades. Jacob's son Joseph, in turn, ends up building such a successful career in real estate in Egypt (Genesis 47) that he cuts off all contact with his home and family and completely assimilates. Only a chance (?) encounter with his brothers awakens his memories—however, he doesn't leave Egypt to return with them to the Promised Land, but brings them all down to Egypt. The rest of the Torah takes place in Egypt and the desert, but most of its text is occupied with planning for the return, with setting forth the outlines of the utopian society and the state the Children of Israel were commanded to create in the Land of Israel.

After about five hundred years, of which only eighty were lived under a unified, sovereign kingdom, including all the tribes, the Israelites were exiled to Babylonia. Although they were given the opportunity, two generations later, to return to the Land of Israel, most of them did not. Instead, they carefully preserved the memories of the Land of Israel as in the verse above. When what autonomy they did manage to reestablish was ended by the Romans, the equilibrium of living as comfortably as possible in the lands of dispersion while working at keeping alive their memories of *Eretz Yisrael* became just that—an equilibrium, a status quo, a routine. East and west, in Baghdad as in Los Angeles, Jews living in the Diaspora have carefully cultivated their memories of a wonderful land, flowing with milk and honey, ringing with David's songs and the snorting of the oxen plowing the rich earth of the Holy Land. While most Jews may have passed up the opportunity to return to the Land of Israel, they never passed up an opportunity to talk about, sing about, reenact, tell their children about, and study the laws pertaining to life there.

And all of this memory work was remarkably successful. While other exiled peoples disappeared, assimilated, were left high and dry when the waves of nostalgia receded, Jews integrated their memories of geography with their religious beliefs and practices, so that while their religion was founded on faith in a uniquely placeless God, with strong elements of universal morality, every prayer and every ritual reminded them of the existence of their own land, constantly reinforcing a collective memory of the place where they belonged.

What kept us alive as a people, perhaps, was having developed this equilibrium of living on two levels, in two places: Physically, we lived in Minsk or Encino. In memory, we lived in Israel. Now you might say that the success of Zionism ended all that, that attaching secular humanism to messianic hope and modern nationalism resulted in the destruction of that equilibrium by creating the real possibility of living a real life in the Israel of here and now. But I think it's not that simple. This is, of course, a wonderful place, flowing, if not with milk and honey, then with high-tech genius and drip-irrigation systems that feed the world. It is a real, sovereign state. But it is not the utopia we were commanded to build; it is not what we remembered all those centuries.

Therefore, I believe that it is more important than ever to keep those memories alive, to restore the equilibrium between memory and reality, between the two homes we live in as Jews. Even now that we have Israel the state, even if we actually live in it—still, if we allow ourselves to forget the Israel we always dreamed of, looking back and looking forward, then the strength of our right hand will be useless and our tongue will have nothing to say.

9. Teaching Israel *(February 18, 2007)*

Palestine is no more of this workday world. It is sacred to poetry and tradition—it is dreamland.

—Mark Twain, *Innocents Abroad* (1869)

Yet, even so, in the material sense the eye of man can distinguish no difference between the land of Israel and any other land; only he who has achieved faith in its holiness can discern a slight difference.

—Rabbi Nachman of Bratslav

If you enter *myths and facts* into an Internet search engine, you'll be flooded with hundreds of pro-Palestinian and pro-Israeli websites, each claiming to separate "facts" from "myths," where *myths* means "lies told by the other side to bolster their moral claims." However, when we talk about *myth* in the realm of Jewish education and Israel engagement, I think we need to be careful to stay away from this simplistic and polemical understanding of the word. The more relevant, and classical, definition of *myth* is a story in which characters and events teach us something about our basic beliefs about humanity and the world. Truth or falsity is not really relevant. The creation myth in Genesis may or may not be accurate in its physics and its biology; however, what it comes to teach us about the order of the universe and our place in it is unaffected by physics. I don't know if Abraham's argument with God over Sodom and Gomorrah really happened as described—but it is a myth from which I am unwilling to part for what it tells me about the relationship among God, humanity, and justice. Of course, in the case of ancient myths, the dilemma of truth versus myth is not so acute, because objective truth is often beyond our reach; we often have no absolute proof that the myth is not really historical truth.

But what about modern myths? It's one thing to say that I can live simultaneously with the creation myth of Genesis and with the findings of paleontologists that suggest that the world as we know it came to be in quite a different way. It's another to say that I can live simultaneously with the myth of Jewish sensitivity to injustice and the findings of social scientists that suggest there is an inordinate amount of corruption and exploitation in Israeli society today.

I find that people's gut reactions to this dissonance fall into two categories:

- Debunk the myth. Let's face it, Jews are no better, morally, than anyone else, and it's not fair to expect them to be. There-fore, why should we be surprised or disappointed by the foibles of the Jewish state? There were Jewish gangsters in Poland and in America; there have been Jewish rapists since the Bible—how is it fair to hold Israel to a higher standard? A myth is only a myth. There wasn't really a flood that destroyed the world, and there isn't really such a thing as Jewish values.

- Deny the reality. Face facts: Jews are smarter and more moral than others. How else can we explain Israel's huge advances in medical care and technology—and all those Palestinian patients at Hadassah Hospital? Of course there are bad apples, but on the whole, Israel is a kinder, gentler society, one big family where people really look out for each other, where you'll never be left uninvited for Shabbat or struggling to change a flat tire by yourself. The troubling headlines on corruption in govern-ment, organized crime, and poverty give a distorted picture of the reality of life here.

I believe there is a third option, which I prefer. As with the cre-ation myth, I understand the myth of Jewish moral superiority not as scientific truth, but as a story that comes to teach me something: Morality is not genetic; it is commanded. We can't assume that Israel will automatically be a better place than other countries—we have to make it so—we have to keep the myth in view on the horizon to which we are heading. I am unwilling to give up the myth of being an ideal state—and I am unable to deny the reality that we're not. The task of Israel education is somehow to convey to our students the challenge of living in the gap, often painful but sometimes ex-hilarating, between myth and reality.

PART II

The Cycle
of the Jewish Year

10. Elul *(August 27, 2006)*

And the seasons they go round and round
And the painted ponies go up and down
We're captive on the carousel of time
We can't return we can only look behind
From where we came
And go round and round and round
In the circle game.

—Joni Mitchell, "The Circle Game,"
Ladies of the Canyon (1970)

The sun rises, and the sun sets—and glides back to where it rises.

Southward blowing, turning northward, ever turning blows the wind; on its rounds the wind returns. All streams flow into the sea, yet the sea is never full . . .

—Ecclesiastes 1:5–7

The talk shows and tabloid headlines are flooded by stories of the aftermath of the Second Lebanese War (two months ago). The endless posturing of the generals and the political leaders, and the retired generals, and the would-be political leaders, and, of course, the pundits.

Did we win or lose? Should we have fought more, or less? Were we adequately prepared? Was there a plan? Are we better off now, or worse off? Is the political leadership to blame, for whatever went wrong, if anything did, or is the military leadership to blame, or is the media to blame? Would anyone else have done things any differently—and if so, how? The questions and recriminations go on and on. In Israeli public discourse we are partial to soul-searching, but we generally prefer that the searching be done in someone else's soul.

And while this noisy, blustery circus plays on, there is also a quiet change going on. Gently, inexorably, just under the radar, Elul has arrived, and is passing day by day, bringing us ever closer back around to Rosh HaShanah. Suddenly (it seems) it is dark when I get up in the morning. And when I walk the dog the rays of the rising sun are sometimes filtered through clouds—which have been absent for months. It is still plenty hot by midmorning, but the light is different, as is the air. There is a humid breeze. Summer fruit (much of which we missed, as it rotted on the trees as katyusha rockets from Lebanon prevented the harvest) tastes like "after the season" except for the melons and grapes that are at their peak now. The pomegranates are bursting on our little tree. One can see on the trees that this year the olive harvest will be a bumper crop. Below the headlines about the repercussions of the war, the annual ritual of school budget cuts, classroom shortages, and, of course, strike threats, appear in the papers, reminding us that the new school year is about to begin (or not). Traditionally, the shofar is sounded every weekday during this month at the *Shacharit* service; we don't have a daily minyan at Shorashim, but my neighbor, who is our shofar blower, practices every morning. Most significant, of course, the *chatzavim* (squill) have shot up their stalks of tiny white flowers—just in case you missed any of the other signs of the season.

Even though, in our climate, fall is a season of hope, as we anticipate the beginning of the rainy season, a green time of growth and renewal, Elul seems to carry a shadow of sadness. Perhaps it is the dimming of the light, the cooling down, the transition to a time that is more changeable, uncertain, unpredictable. I really can't tell how much this feeling is rooted in the spiritual calendar, the sense of impending judgment, of having to face our own soul-searching—and how much is related to the cycle of nature, the seasonal transition, the end of summer. Is it the turning of the spiritual year, or the turning of the seasons that reminds us of our mortality? I suppose that here in Israel the two are really inseparable.

As a religion, dealing with matters of the spirit, in harmony with the cycles of nature, powerless to intervene in the dramatic interplay of nations on the stage of history, Judaism infused the Jews' lives with meaning through centuries of persecution and exile. It has been said that Zionism is about the Jewish people's return to history. Zionism insists that we are a nation, an actor on the stage, with the power to determine our own destiny. Power implies action, action implies consequences, consequences imply responsibility. History is, of course, a great thing, and no one wants to be left out, but at times I feel that it has been overrated. From what I have seen of it, I'm not sure why we were so anxious to get back in the game. Indeed, sometimes just the up-and-down of the carousel of the seasons seems about all I can handle; I'm not sure I have the stomach for the roller coaster of history.

11. Days of Awe: Yom Kippur *(October 1, 2005)*

Our origin is dust and dust is our end. Each of us is a shattered urn, grass that must wither, a flower that will fade, a shadow moving on, a cloud passing by, a particle of dust floating on the wind, a dream soon forgotten.
　　—*Gates of Repentance* (CCAR 1978; revised 1996)

The festivals and the historical holidays, with their dramatic stories and colorful customs, have weathered secularization pretty well. The

High Holy Days, on the other hand, whose main activity is praying in the synagogue, have suffered in the transition from the traditional community to the predominantly secular Jewish state. Yom Kippur, at least, has had an advantage in negotiating the process, a key symbolic behavior that can be secularized: the fast. Many nonobservant Israelis feel an emotional attachment to the tradition of fasting, and have assigned it a humanistic meaning of personal accounting, of taking stock and resolving to improve. However, beyond the fast, I think that many Israeli Jews have struggled to find meaningful and appropriate content for the day. While there are certainly many who go to the beach or travel abroad to escape Yom Kippur, most people feel the need to recognize the day, when, in any case, all normal commercial and cultural activity is shut down. Some go to synagogue for a brief nostalgic or symbolic visit, or to "show the kids." *Kol Nidrei* and *Ne'ilah* (concluding) services are crowded with "tourists" who don't take a prayer book, but just sit there for the experience. The lack of vehicular traffic in most cities has led to a custom of Yom Kippur as "bicycle day." The streets are taken over by kids on bikes by the hundreds, just riding for the sake of riding (and because there is nothing else to do). The next day the media always report the statistics of bike-riding injuries and people hospitalized for dehydration from fasting.

Interestingly, a modern historical event has infused Yom Kippur with a whole new and unexpected meaning that has helped restore its gravity and power for many who had become alienated from its messages and traditions. The surprise attack on Israel launched by Egypt and Syria on Yom Kippur in 1973 and the ensuing bitter and costly war on two fronts was, of course, a national trauma—but now, over three decades later, it seems to have been not only a short-term shock, but a kind of spiritual turning point.

Israel's swift and decisive victory in the Six-Day War of 1967 had left Israelis with a feeling of euphoria and invincibility. We had showed the world and ourselves how strong and clever we really were, and how ridiculous the Arabs' blustering war-mongering really was. We had conquered, easily, huge expanses of land, some of it of symbolic if not cosmic significance (Jerusalem and Hebron, for example) and some of it strategically important (the Golan Heights). No longer would anyone—including ourselves—be able to doubt our continued existence. Then, on Yom Kippur of 1973 we learned a lesson in humility, to say the least. The bubble burst, and the emotional, spiritual impact was devastating.

We Israelis had always trusted our leaders implicitly, especially in matters of defense and security. The army was a key element in our national identity, our answer to two thousand years of powerlessness, the symbol of the New Jew. On Yom Kippur of 1973 we were forced to ask: If we are so smart and so brave and so well-organized and so professional, how were we so vulnerable to a surprise attack that had been months in preparation? Perhaps our leaders were not infallible and our blind faith not well-placed.

And so it happened that Yom Kippur became a day of *national* remembrance and soul-searching, superimposed on its traditional theme of *individual* atonement. A well-known expression of this transition is the story of the melody of the *Un'taneh Tokef* prayer: In 1990, the popular composer Yair Rosenblum was living in Kibbutz Bet Hashittah. He composed a new melody for *Un'taneh Tokef*, dedicated to the memory of the eleven members of the kibbutz who had fallen in the Yom Kippur War. That melody has become a kind of universal anthem of the holiday, used in synagogues of every type, and played on the radio around Yom Kippur. And everyone knows its story. Traditionally, of course, memorial candles are lit and memorial prayers said for loved ones on this day; for many, it has become a national memorial day as well, as thousands of Israelis lost loved ones and friends in that war. The cruel coincidence of the war with Yom Kippur has reinfused a day whose original meaning may have thinned with renewed emotional and spiritual power, forcing us to meditate on the relationship of the individual to the collective, on the meaning of authority, and on the definitions and implications of power and powerlessness.

12. The Smell of the *Etrog*: Sukkot *(October 8, 2006)*

> I believe that the four species are a symbolic expression of our rejoicing that the Israelites exchanged the wilderness, "no place of seed, or of figs, or of vines, or of pomegranates, or of water to drink" (Numbers 20:5), with a country full of fruit trees and rivers. In order to remember this we take the fruit which is the most pleasant of the fruit of the land, branches which smell best, most beautiful leaves, and also the best of herbs. . . .
> —Rambam (Maimonides), *Guide for the Perplexed* 3:43

In previous years, yeshiva students set up a sukkah in the center hall of the old Karmiel Mall for the days between Yom Kippur and Sukkot, where they were the only local source for the "four species"—*etrogim*, palm fronds, myrtle, and willow twigs. As it happened, the space allocated for their booth was right in front of the Diesel boutique, and it always struck me as a funny contrast: the young men in their long-sleeved white shirts and black trousers, doing business right next to the Diesel saleswomen, probably the same age dressed (barely) in halter tops and miniskirts.

But now, the center of Karmiel is fading. The action is moving to a new strip mall in the industrial zone. Perhaps there is some symbolic significance to the fact that this year, the yeshiva boys sold their wares from within the empty Diesel storefront (the sign is still there). The operation was very modest this year for some reason—no tinsel decorations for sale, not even a demonstration sukkah, just a folding table in front of a pile of cartons, displaying half a dozen palm fronds in tinted plastic cases and myrtle twigs sealed in plastic bags. There was one improvement this year: The *etrogim* were not sealed in boxes, but just lying out there in their foam net jackets, to be handled and inspected. Since willow branches don't keep, *lulav* sellers generally don't stock them. Instead, they bring in a big pile of fresh branches on the morning of *erev* Sukkot and they leave them for anyone who wishes to return and take a few. This year, however, we were able to pick our own from a neighbor's yard. The neighbors had planted a willow sapling which, irrigated with graywater (water recycled from sinks and showers), is growing well, saving us a return trip to Karmiel (the biblical verse specifies "willows of the brook"; I wonder if this counts).

For centuries, the best and most prolific sources for *etrogim* were the Greek island of Corfu and the coastal areas of Italy. And in recent years, most of the palm fronds sold in Israel have been imported from Egypt, though apparently this year the Egyptians placed limits on the export of fronds, which was a boon to Israeli date palm growers. Nevertheless, I think the Rambam spoke for most Jews, throughout the ages, who saw this somewhat bizarre practice of waving around a bunch of branches during prayers as a sensory reminder of our connection to *Eretz Yisrael*. Whether you're sitting in Arizona or Siberia, come the fifteenth of Tishrei, the rustle of the palm frond and the fragrance of the *etrog* transport you briefly to a land long ago and far away—yet ever present through experiences like this.

I examined the branches closely through the plastic, trying to look as if I knew what I was doing, and picked a set. From the sparse selection, I chose the least misshapen *etrog*. We have always liked ours yellow, but this year the only decent ones were solid green. A few days later, on the first day of the holiday, I put the four together, said the blessing, shook them in six directions, and instinctively put the *etrog* to my nose for a parting sniff before returning it to its case. I am sure this was the most fragrant *etrog* I have ever encountered. It had a pungency—sweet, tart, refreshing, like the smell of *Eretz Yisrael* itself—that made me want to keep taking deep breaths and not to close the *etrog* away in its case, a smell that left me with a smile for the morning. It was not an orange or a grapefruit or a lemon smell, but the distinctive fragrance of the *etrog*, Jewish oxygen, giving meaning, finally, to the cryptic commandment (Leviticus 23:40) to "take up [the four species] . . . and rejoice."

13. Season's Greetings: Chanukah
(November 25, 2007)

The Chanukah story, in the Book of I Maccabees, opens with Mattathias killing a fellow Jew who agrees to participate in pagan worship, thus declaring a revolt against the Seleucid government and its religious decrees. As much as we would like this holiday to be about pluralism, it is (at least as the story is told in the Book of I Maccabees) about fanaticism. For this reason, and others, it morphed over the years. For the Rabbis, it commemorated the miracle of the oil; for Zionists, it became a festival of nationalism; when I was growing up it was seen by many Jews as our answer to Christmas; for some Jews today, it seems, the focus is not on olive oil, but on saving the world from the consequences of limitless burning of nonrenewable hydrocarbon fuels.

A few hundred years after Mattathias's zealous act, Rabban Gamaliel was bathing in the bath of Aphrodite in Akko (Acre). A pagan challenged him, wondering what the head of the Sanhedrin was doing bathing opposite a statue of a Greek goddess. The Rabbi answered:

> I didn't come into her space, she came into mine: One doesn't say, "Let's build a bathhouse in honor of Aphrodite," but rather, "Let's make an Aphrodite to decorate our bathhouse." . . . The prohibition refers to "their gods": Those that are treated as gods are forbidden; those not treated as gods are permitted.
>
> —*Mishnah Avodah Zarah* 3:4

Even though the Torah is pretty clear about the prohibition against graven images, the oral tradition preserves many important voices that moderate this prohibition in one way or another. Our classical literature is full of different views on the limits of our interaction with the cultures around us.

A dream of modern Zionism (a dream that, I suspect, is still held by many Jews around the world) was that the Jewish state would be as Jewish as European or American cultures were Christian, with Jewish symbols dominating the public space and Jewish holiday songs playing on the sound systems in the elevators. And indeed, so it has come to pass: Israel is Jewish the way America and Europe are Christian. However, it turns out that Europe and America, for all their Christian majority dominance, are today more variegated and pluralistic than a few generations ago. There are Chanukah menorahs in public spaces in the United States, and the Muslim presence is very much felt in Europe. Therefore, for us to be Jewish as they are Christian means that in Israel, too, the reality is more complicated than the myth.

- There was always, of course, a Christian presence here, primarily in Christian Arab communities. I always found it weird to drive through an Arab village, with its distinctively Middle Eastern feel, and encounter illuminated Santa Clauses riding their sleighs over snowless roofs. But over the past two decades, with the large wave of immigration from the former Soviet Union—including both some practicing Christians and some Jews for whom Christmas in the old country was a "cultural, seasonal celebration"—one often sees Christmas decorations in the windows in urban Jewish neighborhoods as well. And the thousands of foreign workers from Europe, South America, Africa, and Asia add to this phenomenon.
- It is two months and ten days between the two main Muslim festivals, Id El Fitr and Id El Adha. As the Muslim lunar

calendar shifts past the solar calendar eleven days a year, every thirty-two years we go through a sequence of about eight years when one of those holidays falls within a few weeks of Chanukah and/or Christmas. Therefore, there is the feeling of one long holiday season that includes everybody—and there are various Festival of Festivals programs here and there around the country.

- And then there is Sylvester, what Israelis call New Year's Day, under the influence of the European tradition of St. Sylvester's Day. For secular Israelis, it's a popular, secular, Western holiday; for the religious, it's a forbidden Christian observance.

This season highlights the gap between the rich cultural reality here and the myth of a place that would be "just Jewish." I don't think Mattathias would approve. But I imagine Rabban Gamaliel would feel just fine.

14. Mother Earth: Tu BiSh'vat *(January 23, 2005)*

More than perhaps any other holiday in the Jewish calendar (even Chanukah), Tu BiSh'vat has been reinvented in modern Israel. For each of the holidays, of course, their modern reincarnations in Israel—even, in many cases, for the Orthodox—include practices and meanings unknown a century ago. In the case of Chanukah, for example, we rehabilitated the Maccabees and their military victory. In the case of Pesach and Shavuot, agricultural motifs took on new life in the people's consciousness. But in the case of Tu BiSh'vat, we essentially created a holiday out of nothing. Originally, the day was barely a blip on the calendar, purely a technical date marking the turn of the year for purposes of calculating tithes (see Mishnah *Rosh HaShanah* 1:1). Kabbalists in sixteenth-century Safed sought and found in it mystical significance, instituting a ceremony of eating and blessing the fruit of trees as a *tikkun* ("repair") to the world that humanity had damaged in the affair of the forbidden fruit in Eden. But this custom remained largely unknown outside that community.

The fifteenth day of the Hebrew month of Sh'vat only became anything like a holiday in the twentieth century, as Zionists seized on it. For example, the prominent historian and educator Joseph Klausner wrote in 1920:

> [Tu BiSh'vat] is a reminder to us that we will not leave father nature and mother earth; that the land is holy in the most exalted religious national sanctity; . . . that in the end, as long as we have a closeness and sensitivity to nature as expressed in the holiday of Tu BiSh'vat, we will be rooted in the soil and all the evil winds that blow on us from all sides will not move us from our place. Let this minor holiday arouse in us the desire to be rooted in our land like a green tree in the earth of its orchard . . . and then the spring will come also for us, then a new year will begin for us as for the trees in our beloved land, after the cold winter of exile.

After centuries of being *luftmenschen,* "air people," living in other people's lands, never at home, always vulnerable, living from commerce (not from the soil like a "normal" people), the Jews had come home. There was probably no image that expressed our image of our new selves more aptly than the tree: rooted deeply in the soil, standing proud (because of those roots) through years of vicissitudes—flood and drought—providing shade, producing useful and beautiful fruit. Trees were everything that exilic Jews were not (in the Zionist imagination). And so Tu BiSh'vat was tuned exactly to the right pitch; it celebrated our being born anew with a different kind of identity. The newly invented custom of planting trees on Tu BiSh'vat changed the poetic imagery to an action, a Zionist mitzvah that linked together building the new society, restoring the land and ourselves, and showing faith in the future.

The kabbalistic custom of eating a number of different fruits in a specific mystical order—the Tu BiSh'vat seder—was resurrected by educators in the second half of the twentieth century, and in recent years has become extremely popular in Israel. In preparing a seder for a group of teachers this year, I included Klausner's words, but then had second thoughts. The fierce debate in Israel today between those who support the disengagement from Gaza (and the ultimate withdrawal from other territories occupied in 1967), and those who oppose it often revolves around rhetoric exactly like Klausner's. Today the division in Israel can be understood as between those who sanctify the land and those who sanctify the state, between those who say the (divinely ordained) duty to be rooted in the land transcends the duty to obey the law of the temporal state, even if it is a Jewish state, and those who say that "The law of the state is the law."

On the one hand, Tu BiSh'vat has lost some of its innocence. It is hard to separate its spiritual message (with its romantic nationalist overtones) from the harsh tones of politics. On the other hand, if you don't want to be a *luftmensch,* you have to get your hands dirty.

15. Purim Reflections *(March 23, 2008)*

Esther did not reveal her people or her kindred, for Mordecai had told her not to reveal it.

—Esther 2:10

And many of the people of the land professed to be Jews, for the fear of the Jews had fallen upon them.

—Esther 8:17

Once when I was the part-time weekend rabbi of a very small congregation in a small town in the Midwest, I unwittingly created a furor by acquiescing to a congregant's request that I write a letter to the local school board asking to tone down the Christmas observance in the public schools. In the end, the leadership of the congregation repudiated me and my letter, as my action constituted a threat to their longstanding modus vivendi as a minority in the town. I guess I should have been more sensitive—after all, I had played Santa Claus in the fourth-grade play, and my parents were very proud.

I was reminded of these experiences this week when Tami reported seeing an Arab mother in the grocery store in Karmiel on Purim, wearing the head scarf of a religious Muslim, with her little boy dressed in a Spider-Man costume. This was consistent with her experience at work, at the day-care center for handicapped children at the hospital in Nahariya, where Purim was celebrated with great glee, with costumes and songs and hamentaschen by the kids and the staff, who reflect the population of the region, 80 percent Arab.

I suppose Purim is analogous to Halloween—Halloween (All Hallows' Eve) is a pagan holiday that was taken over by the Christians, and is based on beliefs that are certainly foreign to Judaism—which doesn't stop most American Jewish kids from trick-or-treating, having Halloween parties, and investing great effort in dressing up. I suspect that very few Christians and pagans give much thought to the deep meaning of the day beyond the "values" of masquerading and candy; the only people who remember the original content are Orthodox Jews who decline to participate in the fun. Similarly, it seems you can be a religious Muslim and buy your kid a Spider-Man costume for Purim without delving into the Book of Esther with its various possible interpretations regarding exile, identity, power, and providence. You probably can spin the Purim story to support pluralism and brotherhood, but you have to spin pretty hard, especially chapters 8 and 9. Thus, it seems that Purim has become a seasonal holiday in Israel in the same way that Halloween (and even Christmas and Easter) have become seasonal holidays in

North America—secular cultural events seemingly disconnected from their original religious meaning. Their observances (Spider-Man, chocolate bunnies, colored lights, and candy canes) have lost, for many people, any connection to religious content; they have become symbols whose referents have vanished in the transition from religion to folklore.

Those of us engaged in Jewish education have always seen this blurring of religious meaning as a negative development, a sign of assimilation, of diminution of Jewish knowledge and commitment, a fading of Jewish identity. But here's an interesting question: If Zionism envisioned a Judaism that was reconceptualized as a national culture, not a religion, should we not be happy to see citizens of Israel of other religions who feel comfortable with that national culture? Could it be that Muslim Spider-Men on Purim are signs of the success of secular Zionism in creating an Israeli (as opposed to Jewish) national culture. Or should we see other people's assimilation as just as distressing as our own?

16. Pesach: Leaving the Desert Behind
(March 15, 2009)

Encamped at Gilgal, in the steppes of Jericho, the Israelites offered the Passover sacrifice on the fourteenth day of the month, toward evening. On the day after the Passover offering, on that very day, they ate of the produce of the country, unleavened bread and parched grain. On the same day, when they ate of the produce of the land, the manna ceased. The Israelites got no more manna; that year they ate of the yield of the land of Canaan.

—Joshua 5:10–12

We learn in chapter 5 of Joshua that while the generation of the Exodus had been circumcised in Egypt, their children and grandchildren born in the desert had not. And since only the circumcised may eat of the Passover sacrifice, it seems that this ritual, too, was not maintained during the forty years in the desert. Anyway, the Israelites couldn't have eaten matzah in the desert as they had no grain—only manna. Thus, the first Passover in the Land of Israel was rather a significant event, a new experience for the people. We generally think of Pesach as the feast of liberation, a commemoration of our going forth from Egypt into the desert. However, it turns out that Pesach "bookends" the desert experience—on Pesach the Children of Israel left slavery for the desert, and on Pesach they celebrated leaving the desert and taking responsibility for sustaining and governing themselves in their new land.

> And when you enter the land that the Eternal will give you, as promised, you shall observe this rite. And when your children ask you, "What do you mean by this rite?" you shall say, "It is the passover sacrifice to the Eternal, who passed over the houses of the Israelites in Egypt when smiting the Egyptians, but saved our houses."
>
> —Exodus 12:25–27

It is interesting to try to imagine the questions that might have been asked at that moment of transition from desert exile to settled sovereignty—at the first seder in the land:

- On all the other nights of all the years of our lives we ate manna, which had the quality of tasting like whatever we wanted it to taste like (e.g., lobster); why tonight do we eat only this dry matzah?
- On all other nights we ate food that fell from heaven—all we had to do was gather it; why tonight do we only eat bread that is the product of our labors of cultivation and preparation?
- On all other nights we sat on our suitcases; why tonight have we unpacked?

- On all other nights we drank water from Miriam's miraculous portable well; how on this night will we stay awake if all we have to drink is the wine of the grapes of the Land of Israel?
- On all other nights we were surrounded and protected by the endless desert; why tonight do we sit with our doors open to listen for any suspicious activity by our new neighbors?
- On all other nights we were all equal, sustained by God's providence; why tonight are there poor among us for whom we must take responsibility?
- On all other nights we knew we could rely on Moses to lead us; why tonight is our dinner-table conversation about the crisis of leadership?
- On all other nights we looked out of our tents at an endless and unknown wilderness; why tonight does every hill and valley, every rock and tree suddenly have a name and a meaning for us?
- On all other nights, when we felt that we belonged someplace, it was Egypt; why tonight do we feel we belong here?
- On all other nights we could ask our parents about their memories of slavery and redemption; how on this night shall we answer our children's questions?
- On all other nights we worried about getting to the Land of Israel; why tonight do we worry about being allowed to stay here?
- On all other nights, we studied the Torah as a theoretical exercise, relevant to some distant future; why tonight does the transition from theory to practice seem so overwhelming?
- On all other nights, it was the older generation that was responsible for our predicament; why on this night are we suddenly responsible for ourselves?
- On all other nights, we dreamed of coming into our own land, that had been promised to us; of what shall we dream tonight?

17. Memory: Yom HaShoah and Yom HaZikaron
(*May 15, 2005*)

"Your glory, O Israel,
Lies slain on your heights;
How have the mighty fallen!"

—II Samuel 1:19

David's beautiful and moving eulogy for Saul and Jonathan has become the standard text for military eulogies, and is often recited at modern Israeli funerals and memorial observances. This is memorial season in Israel: On the last day of Pesach, traditionally, the morning service includes *Yizkor*, the memorial service for all of our loved ones no longer with us; a few days later comes Yom HaShoah and, a week later, Yom HaZikaron, the memorial day for Israel's war dead (and now also for those killed in terrorist attacks). As spring gives way to summer, the land warms up and dries out. We switch our life rhythm to Daylight Savings Time. The school year winds down. It is a time of bittersweet transition. We stop and look back. We stop and remember those who have fallen, those who helped make us who we are, both personally and nationally. We pause to consider, if only for a fleeting moment, that now, without them, we are somehow less than we once were or might someday have been.

Yom HaShoah and Yom HaZikaron are secular rituals that have developed an orthodoxy of their own. On each day, air raid sirens go off throughout the country at a set hour (on Yom HaShoah, at 11 A.M.; on Yom HaZikaron, at 8 P.M. and 11 A.M.). All of us are expected to stop whatever we are doing and stand at attention for the duration of the siren. It's always awkward if you are driving and don't have the radio on and it takes you a minute to figure out why all the cars are pulling over and people are getting out. And, of course, the tabloids love to expose the anti-Zionist ultra-Orthodox Jews or Arabs who ignored the siren.

The radio operates, but only broadcasts lugubrious music, while the TV broadcasts Holocaust movies or features on war heroes. Of course, if you happen to turn to a foreign station via satellite or cable, it is business as usual.

Schools and communities hold memorial ceremonies that are generally highly formulaic and ritualized: The readers standing in a line in white shirts, the nonfunctional sound system, the well-known poems and descriptive passages, read with sad earnestness but often not really heard or understood by the congregation/audience; a few sad songs; a memorial prayer. On Yom HaShoah there are the six candles; on Yom HaZikaron the Israeli custom of "fire script"—the word *yizkor* (remember) spelled out in oil-soaked rags on a wire frame and set alight. And then, after the ceremony, people socialize awkwardly, not sure if it's the right thing to do, but not quite ready to go home. Sometimes there are moments that genuinely call forth tears; sometimes it is, like any ritual, "just" a ritual that we know we have to do, with or without feeling.

For me, these days provide an opportunity to reflect on how we construct and sanctify our collective memories. What we choose to remember and to ritualize says something about who we think we are and who we want our children to be. The scheduling of Yom HaShoah and Yom HaZikaron a week apart has, perhaps, a meaning of its own: In the Holocaust, we were the world's ultimate victims, powerless—history happened to us. In Israel's wars, we died in the process of exercising our power, as full and equal players on the stage of history. In both cases, we remember those who died because they were Jews. And yet the memories are very different.

The Pesach Haggadah says that in every generation we must see ourselves as though we personally had come forth from Egypt— and now, perhaps, as though we rode the train to Auschwitz and withstood the Syrian onslaught in the Golan in 1973. The currency of memory has not depreciated through centuries of Passover seders. I wonder if our newly invented rituals will be as enduring.

18. Tishah B'Av *(July 21, 2002)*

Because of this our hearts are sick, because of these our eyes
  are dimmed:
Because of Mount Zion, which lies desolate; jackals prowl over
  it.
But You, O Lord, are enthroned forever, Your throne endures
  through the ages.
Why have you forgotten us utterly, forsaken us for all time?
Take us back, O Lord, to Yourself, and let us come back; renew
  our days as of old.
For truly, You have rejected us, bitterly raged against us.
                                              —Lamentations 5:19–22

The Ninth of Av in Jerusalem—the first time I've been here on this day in at least twenty years. We arrive at Zion Gate of the old city at around 8 P.M. and walk through the Jewish quarter to the Western Wall plaza. Apparently, it is early, as there seem to be no other worshipers around—just hundreds of police and soldiers, milling around, fooling around, lounging on the staircases, unpacking equipment from fleets of vehicles, passing around Styrofoam cups of coffee. There is something ominous about this massive armed presence in the deserted streets of Jerusalem. We pass through a security checkpoint at the entrance to the plaza, similar to that at the airport (but no boarding pass).

In previous years, attempts to hold services with a mixed congregation of men and women anywhere in the plaza have resulted in violent responses by some of the ultra-Orthodox, attempts to pass laws in the Knesset forbidding such "sacrilege," and police refusal to sanction or guard those participating in such gatherings. However, a compromise has been reached: Over the past few decades, archaeologists have uncovered the continuation of the wall of the Temple Mount south of the plaza that was created just after the 1967 war. Thus, the exposed portion of the Western Wall of the Mount is now at least twice as long as what is depicted in pictures and maps showing the Western Wall and its plaza. This more recently excavated portion is separated from the plaza by the ramp leading up to a gate to the Temple Mount itself, and is fenced off as part of an antiquities park. So while it is no less ancient, authentic, and holy than the area traditionally labeled as the Western Wall, this southern section has escaped being included in the jurisdiction of the ultra-Orthodox keepers of the Wall. The police permit the non-Orthodox to use this area to hold holiday services according to their beliefs, and the ultra-Orthodox pay no attention.

We join those assembling at the entrance to the southern wall excavations, and when the group reaches critical mass, we are allowed to enter and organize. There are about one hundred people, with a heavy representation of Anglos—American rabbinical students and immigrants like me—plus a busload of recent immigrants from the former Soviet Union, many of whom are making their first visit to Jerusalem. Chapters of Lamentations had been assigned in advance to readers with good voices, so the book is beautifully chanted and easy to follow (I forgot a flashlight, but fortunately brought a prayer book with large-print text). The floodlit wall towering over us, the familiar melody of the chant of Lamentations, the police helicopters and blimps circling overhead, the heterogeneous congregation scattered among the ruins—all this changes the atmosphere from ominous to surreal.

By the time we finish the reading and emerge back into the plaza, the place is packed, and people are continuing to stream in from all entrances. In the 1970s, gathering at the Wall on Tishah B'Av was a social and cultural event that attracted Jerusalemites and visitors of all backgrounds. The famous tour guide Zeev Vilnai used to lead a walk along the perimeter wall. Those visiting the Wall were almost joyful—the day of mourning over our loss of the city had been turned into a celebration of our return to it. Over the years, however, the atmosphere and the crowd have changed. The secular celebrants of return have given the Wall back to mourners of the destruction.

The entire plaza is covered with circles of men, sitting on the ground listening to the chant of Lamentations and of medieval dirges composed for this day. Each circle represents a different community, a different ethnic tradition, a different melody. And circulating among them, hundreds of beggars, both amateur and professional.

The experience of the evening reminds me of my own ambivalence about this day, as I consider the conflicting feelings it arouses. There is a dissonance between the religious obligation to mourn with tearful recitation of dirges the loss of our sovereignty in our land, and the reality that we are sovereign in our land—even more than we were through most of the Second Temple period. Are we really in exile today? The texts of the day express longing for the restoration of the Temple cult, but the fact is that I am not really looking forward to a return to a religion in which a hereditary priesthood presides over worship based on animal sacrifice. There is, of course, the option of abandoning the day as no longer relevant. However, is it really no longer relevant? Is this the redemption for which we waited so many centuries? Somehow I can't avoid the feeling that wherever it is we are going, we are not there yet, that mourning for our political and spiritual loss is a valid expression of our longing for a perfected state in a perfected world—and a reminder of our obligation to work for it.

I love living in the Galilee—a place that has its own rich history and sites of spiritual significance. And I'm not sure I believe that God's presence is closer or stronger at the Western Wall—or that God reads the notes people place in the cracks. But there is something in the atmosphere there, an echo of history, an intensity, that explains its role as a pilgrimage destination. The reflections stimulated by my visit there will stay with me after my return home to the periphery, as every pilgrimage leaves a spiritual residue in the pilgrim.

PART III

Reflections on Community

19. Community and State *(February 22, 2004)*

A learned person (*talmid chacham*) is not permitted to live in
a city that does not have the following ten things: a court; a
tzedakah fund; a synagogue; a *mikveh;* sufficient bathroom
facilities; a doctor; a blood-letter; a scribe; a butcher; a Torah
teacher for children.

— Babylonian Talmud, *Sanhedrin* 17b

Zionism can be seen as a response to a number of different historical developments at the end of the nineteenth century. According to
the classic story of Theodor Herzl's epiphany while reporting on the
Dreyfus trial, Zionism was a way to deal with the intractability of
European anti-Semitism and the collapse of the enlightenment dream
of a neutral society. A more sociological analysis sees the movement as a synthesis of traditional messianism, secular humanism,
and European romantic nationalism. From a different perspective,
Zionism appears to be a response to the breakdown of the traditional Jewish community. The rise of the modern state meant the
end of the semiautonomous Jewish community, ruling itself largely
by Torah law and rabbinic authority. Emancipation meant that Jews

became individual citizens of the state without the mediation of the Jewish community, and the community therefore lost its authority and its centrality in Jewish identity. The community contracted to the status of a voluntary association with minimal powers, dealing mainly with education, culture, and family, relinquishing most civil authority to the state.

The Zionist response to the collapse of community was twofold. On the one hand the state became the replacement for community. If the traditional European ghetto was "a state within a state," the Zionist dream was a state in its own right. In the Zionist state we would have not only autonomy, but full sovereignty and independence. Combining nostalgia for the biblical image of a Jewish state with an idealized view of the ethnic nation-states of early twentieth-century Europe, Jews imagined themselves liberated from the ghetto/community into the new, redeemed reality of the Jewish state.

On the other hand, from the beginning of large-scale Jewish settlement here in the late nineteenth century, the Land of Israel has seen a constant series of experiments in the creation of communities that would restore aspects of what was lost in the transition to the modern state. The best known of these, of course, is the kibbutz. We tend to think of the kibbutz as an experiment in pure socialism, but the economic structure was only part of the story. The debates that raged through the kibbutzim and their associations over the century have dealt less with economics and more with social issues: the optimum size for the community; the status of women; family obligations; the responsibility for raising the children. And while the kibbutz movement was struggling to define its ideal community, other models were created: the *moshav shitufi*, in which the economy is communal, but the family unit remains largely autonomous (there is no communal dining room or laundry or children's quarters); the *moshav ovdim*, a farming village, where only certain equipment and services are communal; and now, the ubiquitous *yishuv kehilati*, or "community settlement," which is essentially a residential village—usually with only minimal employment opportunities, so that most residents commute to work elsewhere. Today the kibbutz is struggling to define itself anew and privatization seems to be an irresistible force sweeping through all forms of collective communities. The atomizing forces of mass culture and globalization are pounding at the gates. Liberation, it turns out, is a two-edged sword, for while the traditional community had come to seem stifling and limiting, cutting us off from the modernizing society around us, it was the community that defined our Jewish identity and supported it. Transferring that function to a state has turned out to be more complicated than we thought, and is the root cause, I believe, of the ongoing conflict regarding the status of religion in Israel. When Judaism is defined by communities—and there are many communities coexisting, separated by geography, ethnicity, historical experience, and leadership styles—then Judaism develops along various paths, sometimes parallel, sometimes colliding, and pluralism is a fact of life. But when the communal functions of defining identity, interpreting Jewish law, and preserving traditions are taken over by the central authority of the state, then pluralism gives way to the ongoing conflict over the one correct interpretation. There can be lots of Jewish communities, and Jews have always moved among them. There is only one Jewish state.

The challenge of the second century of Zionism is to create a sustainable equilibrium and division of labor and authority among community, state, and religion.

20. Kibbutz *(October 10, 2002)*

You want to take root and stay forever in the most temperate and blue of temperate places. Many years of digging and tending made these orchards. Relaxing, breathing freely, you feel

what a wonderful place has been created here, a homeplace for
body and soul.
—Saul Bellow, *To Jerusalem and Back: A Personal Account*
(Penguin Books, 1976)

Last week I was invited to teach an enrichment class for a kibbutz
ulpan (intensive Hebrew class). When I first made *aliyah* I used to
give a lot of lectures like this, but this was the first one I would be
giving in several years. One reason for the lag in my lecturing is that
in the past few years the number of young people coming from the
Diaspora to study in kibbutz *ulpanim* has plummeted, just as every
other tourist enterprise has, as tourism levels reflect perceptions
about security in Israel. Another reason is that as kibbutzim move
toward capitalist economic structures, they are more stringent in
weighing each activity as a profit center, and tend to cut away those
projects, no matter how traditional, that do not generate profits.
Hence, the *ulpan,* which was always borderline economically and
was maintained as much for ideology and idealism as for economic
benefit, has often been a victim of the rationalization and privatization processes.

But there are some *ulpanim* left; the one I visited is at a large old
kibbutz on the edge of the Jezreel Valley. There were about twenty
students at my lecture, all twenty-somethings, ranging from college
dropouts trying to figure out what to do with their lives, to partners
of Israelis preparing for conversion, to seekers and roots-diggers and
time-fillers of all kinds. Most were North Americans, but the group
included volunteers from Turkey, Japan, Sweden, Austria, and Russia as well. They study Hebrew half the day and volunteer in the
kibbutz half the day, and are provided with occasional lectures and
excursions for general education and cultural enrichment. So there
I was, assigned to give an introduction to Judaism in seventy-five
minutes. I focused on the development of the tradition, from Mount
Sinai to the present, discussed the variations in the mainstream of

Jewish belief, and explained the beliefs and origins of the various movements in Judaism today. The students were attentive and enthusiastic and full of thoughtful questions, and a good time was had by all, including me. It always feels good to teach people stuff they really want to know.

As I was leaving, the kibbutz families were all gathering in the communal sukkah for some kind of party. The lawn was crowded with parents and young children, the sidewalks a jam of bikes and trikes and electric carts. It was dusk outside, but the sukkah (not kosher, but symbolic—a compound made by enclosing the open patio located under the dining hall with walls of palm fronds) was brightly lit and colorfully decorated, music was playing, and the scene was very inviting.

Once, images of the kibbutz were used to symbolize the whole of Israel. The reborn Jewish state was credited with creating the first successful utopian communities in history. Many people were shocked to discover that only 2–3 percent of Israelis lived on kibbutzim. In the past decade, works of literature, films, and plays have tended to depict the kibbutz in a negative light, as a place in which individuality is stifled and the family was disassembled. Once, of course, the political elite of the country had roots in the kibbutz movement, which may help to explain the centrality of the kibbutz in Israel's image in the first decades of the state. But that elite has lost its hold—and so has the romantic vision of the kibbutz as utopia.

Anyone who talks to kibbutzniks or reads the paper knows that the kibbutzim are a mess: Young people leave, privatization is advancing, and agriculture is declining. Ten years ago the last kibbutz to retain separate sleeping quarters for children gave in and changed over to having family accommodations. The latest struggle has been over the dining hall; many now have meal tickets, others are open only for certain meals, still others have closed altogether. Everyone knows about the quarrels and backbiting, the lack of privacy and the discouragement of initiative. Everyone knows that the kibbutz is not what it used to be—and probably never was. But it was a useful myth and a beautiful one, and it is hard to let go of it.

When I visit a long-established kibbutz, which I do fairly often, it is usually brief, for a few hours or days, to teach or stay in the guest-house. My experience is not of collapse, but of lush public gardens and broad lawns and public art, of richly equipped playgrounds, of people whose community, family, workplace, and home are all so intertwined that they can spend the whole day in their bedroom slippers. To the outsider it feels warm and comfortable, green and safe. The feel of the kibbutz plucks a string of nostalgia, a memory of what Israel was supposed to be, even if the good old days are, in fact, merely a construct of our collective imagination. After his visit to a kibbutz, Saul Bellow wrote of it as a "homeplace." Indeed, that is what we are supposed to be doing in this land—creating a "home-place for body and soul."

Most people don't feel this way about the kibbutz. That was then, this is now. Cynicism is in. Entrepreneurs are our heroes, and the *equal* distribution of resources is not necessarily the *fairest* one (what about rewarding hard work, for example?). And so I found it refreshing to encounter the *ulpan* volunteers, coming to find themselves, Judaism, and Israel—on a kibbutz.

21. Which Way to Utopia? (March 17, 2002)

> He (Hillel) used to say, "If I am not for myself, who will be for me? And, if I am for myself alone, then what am I? And, if not now, when?"
>
> —*Pirkei Avot* 1:14

The other night I met with representatives of the remnants of the Shorashim collective to renegotiate our lease on the prefab "cara-vans" we use for our hostel. The meeting brought back a host of not-so-pleasant memories of the privatization process that we went through here ten years ago.

When we arrived at Shorashim, it was a *moshav shitufi,* a socialist commune similar to a kibbutz but with a greater degree of personal independence and freedom (e.g., no communal dining room or laundry). Each family placed all its earned income into the common account and received a house, a living allowance based on family size, and at least partial coverage of other various needs like health care, culture, and education. The community owned five businesses; most people worked in those businesses, but it was possible to work outside the moshav and deposit your paycheck in the common account. While a significant amount of time was spent on discussions of what the community should and should not pay for, and while the system did indeed make it too easy to take risks and too easy to avoid responsibility (it seems that it's a lot easier to run up a large collective debt that psychologically, at least, belongs to no one, than it is to run up a large personal debt for which you yourself are fully responsible), on the whole we found it liberating, and liked the ethic of mutual responsibility upon which it was based. Moreover, the communal economy encouraged and subsidized a vibrant community life, something that was very attractive to those of us without extended family in Israel: The community became our extended family.

But then, within a few months of our arrival, we began to hear the rumblings of discontent: the frustrations of people nearing forty years of age after having spent ten years together. They had no savings to show for their time in the moshav, and plenty of debt. We heard of the burnout from endless general assemblies and committees and the feeling that the world was passing the community by. Even the USSR was privatizing. Within two years, a minority who had had enough of socialism had worn down the majority, and we voted — not unanimously — to privatize. We sold off the communal businesses and started a process of parceling the land and arranging the private purchase of the homes. The process took almost ten years to complete.

One of the arguments against privatization had been that it would weaken the community: Members would be less motivated and too busy making a living to spend time and energy on communal activities. And, indeed, holiday observances have gotten simpler, to say the least; the culture committee has collapsed; there is, on the whole, a lot less togetherness and people spend more time working. I know that there is a limit to the amount of control and intense togetherness that middle-class families can take, but nevertheless, I feel something special and valuable was lost in the transition.

The transition turned out to be a fuzzy, slow, circuitous process that is, to this day, not complete. Not only did we have to contend with a bevy of government bureaucracies that didn't know how to handle what has become an increasingly common situation, but we ourselves harbored all kinds of ambivalent feelings about the privatization, which is why the relationships between the various legal entities (the original commune, the new municipal association, and the moshav businesses that were purchased by members as private enterprises) are still being sorted out ten years later. Some of the most enthusiastic supporters of privatization ended up being surprised and not entirely happy with some of its implications.

It turns out that our little hilltop community is a microcosm of Israel at large, as privatization affects everything from the smallest kibbutz to national institutions.

Socialism and Zionism can both be seen as messianic movements, each seeking a once-and-for-all revolution that will be redemptive. Socialist Zionism sought to start the redemption of the world by building utopia in Israel. But times change and utopias lose their glitter (remember Camelot?). The *tikkun olam* idealism of the socialist pioneers who dominated the culture and politics of the country until 1977 has now given way to the worship of entrepreneurship. I don't know if this is a good thing or not. I do know that today, in Israel, the country that gave the world the kibbutz, the gap between the rich and the poor is among the largest and most glaring of any

Western country. I'm sure it was an exaggeration to see socialism as the messiah, but it's not clear that capitalism is a better candidate for the role.

22. Community and Obligation *(March 7, 2004)*

One who gives to *tzedakah* less than his capability—the court may force him to give by means of lashes, or may attach his property.

—Rambam (Maimonides), *Mishneh Torah*,
Gifts to the Poor 7:10

Participation in a funeral may be forced in the same way as *tzedakah* may be forced.

—Rambam (Maimonides), *Mishneh Torah*, Mourning 14:3

Our regional community center has been running a series of workshops titled "Culture Builds Community." The idea is to create a "culture network" among the thirty rural communities (moshavim, kibbutzim, villages) in the county, so that local leaders and planners can share ideas and resources, combine forces, publicize programs efficiently, and thus build a stronger sense of community among all the residents of the county. I have attended several of these sessions, and have gone through a series of reactions and realizations.

A great deal of time is spent complaining to each other about our frustration that no matter how hard we work, no matter how intense the publicity, and no matter how much we spend to bring in big-name lecturers and musicians, the attendance at the events is often disappointing. Not only is attendance low from the region, but participation is disappointing even from the local community that sponsors the event. Everyone has heard complaints from a neighbor after a disappointing turnout for an event in which we had invested heavily of ourselves. Among those complaints: "Why don't you publicize these events?" or worse, "It's a shame there's no cultural life around here."

There seems to be a consensus among community representatives that the problem is one of marketing. If there were a more effective means of getting the word out—if we had a joint website, for example—then our events would draw the attendance they deserve. However, I have my doubts about this assumption, and wonder if perhaps the problem is our consumerist model of culture: We are defining culture as "events" and measuring their success by ticket sales. We are offering a product, marketing it, and selling it to individual consumers who drive in, enjoy their purchase, and drive home. This is a pretty narrow definition of culture and hardly seems like an effective way to build community. It seems to me that culture should be seen not as a product to be purchased, but as a whole network of human interactions based on shared symbols (words, music, pictures, etc.). Part of the appeal of going to a concert is enjoying the music. But part of it is supporting musicians and being with other people enjoying the same music.

One community that does not seem to experience the same frustration is the Orthodox settlement in our county. That community seems to have a vibrant social and cultural life, with a rich schedule of well-attended lectures, concerts, and classes on a wide range of topics. Are they more social? More cultured? Do they have more free time? What's the secret?

My theory is that a key element that makes a community a community is *obligation*. Perhaps a community is fundamentally a network of obligations. In other words, we tend to do what we feel we have to do, not what we feel like doing. In an Orthodox community, daily attendance at a minyan is driven primarily, I think, not by the spiritual "lift" felt by the attendees, but by the belief that this is something we are obligated—even commanded—to do. Indeed, the requirement of a minyan for certain prayers and ceremonies suggests that community is not only essential in Judaism, but also obligatory.

There are certain prayers that are not considered effective or acceptable if recited alone, without a community. That obligation can be sensed as a divine commandment—or as the feeling that the other members of the community are depending on us to be sure there are ten, or to share in the burden of setting up the chairs, learning the Torah reading, and so on. We go even when we don't happen to feel like it, because we feel like we have to.

Moreover, I would suggest that the force of interpersonal obligation in a community is influenced by the frequency and intensity of the contact among the members. If I see my neighbor at minyan every morning, I am less likely to skip the concert he organizes than I would be if my only interaction with him is through the flyer publicizing the event.

On a smaller scale, this theory is borne out at Shorashim, too: There seems to be a high degree of overlap between the group of synagogue regulars who see each other every week at Shabbat services—and who tend to come even when it's raining—and the frequent participants in nonreligious social and cultural events. When you feel the community has a claim on you, it cuts across different spheres of interest and activity. Similarly, when Shorashim was still a commune and most of us worked together every day, attendance at social and cultural events was extremely high, though intuitively, one might have expected that we would want to get away from the group on our free time.

Obligation builds community. The challenge—for rural communities in Israel as, I suspect, for Reform synagogues in North America—is how to generate and preserve a sense of obligation.

23. Freedom of Association *(February 29, 2004)*

Do not bring any and every man to your home.
—Wisdom of Ben Sira 11:29

When we decided to make *aliyah* in 1990, Shorashim was a *moshav shitufi* of about thirty families. The community was run as a pure democracy, one vote per adult. It really didn't seem strange to us that before becoming members we would have to pass the following stages: a preliminary visit, a weeklong trial residency with work, an interview, psychological testing, a vote of the membership to accept us for a year's probation, and a vote to accept us at the end of that year, by a two-thirds majority. Because the community was a commune, in which members were interdependent economically, that process seemed appropriate. Nor did we give much thought to the fact that the whole process was predicated on our being married, Jewish, and under forty (actually, we weren't under forty, and a special vote was required to waive that requirement in our case). After all, there was nothing out of the ordinary about Shorashim's demands: The constitution was a standard document used by virtually all other such communities in Israel (except that on a kibbutz, singles are also accepted).

Then, two years later, Shorashim privatized, disbanding the collective; we were no longer economically interdependent. Thus, the extreme care we took in selecting prospective members began to seem a little excessive. Nevertheless, as we learned from the endless stream of house-hunting young families driving in on Shabbat looking for a modest suburban lifestyle, if we let down our guard we could easily be overwhelmed with people who found our attempt to be a liberal religious community simply a nuisance. What would become of the special Shabbat atmosphere? The communal holiday celebrations? The sensitivity to different people's diverse religious needs? The strong sense of community that meant so much to us? And so, while the procedures were made less draconian with privatization, the basically exclusive nature of the community remained in place.

Twice in the past fourteen years a family did not pass their admission vote. In one case, they had made it clear that they were not joiners and that they were not going to be involved in the religious, cultural, or social life of the community; in the other case, many neighbors had concerns that the family's internal problems would become a burden on the community. Both left hurt and angry.

In the past few years, several families have taken other communities to court over such rejections; in one case, it was an Arab family, where the reason for rejection was their ethnic identity. Other cases have involved rejections based on personal qualities or economic considerations. In all of them, the courts struck down the admissions policies as discriminatory. Many people argue that to force a rural settlement to accept anyone who applies—and especially, to accept Arabs—will mean the end of the Zionist settlement enterprise. And certainly, if a group of people established a community of a particular character, it seems somehow unfair for them to be helpless to prevent that character from being submerged or subverted.

Professor Asa Kasher, a well-known ethicist in Israel, has suggested that there is a conflict between two basic rights:

- the right to live wherever I want, and
- the right to live with whomever I want.

We know from the Jewish experience in America and elsewhere that the right to live with whomever I want sounds good, but is a slippery slope leading to "No Jews or blacks need apply." And indeed, Tami and I are finding that what seemed obvious to us fourteen years ago seems a little bizarre today. Growing up as Jews in the United States, exclusionary communities were anathema. How can we take them for granted as part of the Israeli landscape? As we have matured along with Shorashim—and Israel—we find ourselves questioning the previously sacred assumption that a homogeneous community is a value that supersedes individual freedom. It is a vexing dilemma: What price will we pay for opening the gates? What price will we pay for not opening them?

24. Locked Out—Or Locked In? *(May 11, 2003)*

> The Gazans learned that Samson had come there, so they gathered and lay in ambush for him in the town gate. . . . At midnight, he got up, grasped the doors of the town together with the two gateposts, and pulled them out along with the bar. He placed them on his shoulders and carried them off to the top of the hill that is near Hebron.
>
> —Judges 16:2–3

> Inscribe [these words] on the doorposts of your house and on your gates.
>
> —Deuteronomy 6:9

When we arrived at Shorashim in 1990, there were sections of the perimeter of the settlement that were fenced with several strands of rusty barbed wire measuring approximately four feet in height, the type of fencing used to keep out cows. There was a gate that could be swung shut across the entrance road, and all males had to do guard duty about once a month from midnight to five in the morning. The gate was left open and unguarded except during those five hours. Occasionally, there was a flurry of concern about a stolen bicycle or garden tool, annoyance about the cows ruining our gardens, and ambivalence about the local Arabs collecting wild herbs on our hillside; but otherwise, no one lost any sleep due to fear of intruders. When the community was first established in the mid-1980s, they had requested a perimeter fence, but the Defense Ministry did not feel it was a priority.

Then, around 1995, we were informed that the Defense Ministry had finally found the resources, and we were to receive a perimeter patrol road with lights, and a proper seven-foot chain-link fence topped with barbed wire. Some of us were relieved, others annoyed by this intrusion into the landscape. When the objectors tried to make an issue of it, they were informed that it was too late, as the contract to install the fence had already been signed. The only concession that we were able to extract was to reduce the height to five feet.

And so the bulldozers cut a path around the mountain, apparently not always working according to a blueprint, as the patrol road strayed off into several dead ends. Wooden poles were erected for sodium vapor lights aimed outwards, and the fence was stretched along the road. The topography of the mountain is such that there are several large gaps where the fence could not be built. Thus, while it is quite effective in preventing us from hiking around the mountainside, it seems to be less effective in keeping cows and goats out. Moreover, as one would expect, the inconvenience of the fence for shepherds and hikers led, within a couple of years, to the appearance of several unofficial "openings" allowing passage between Shorashim and the open mountainside. We still have cows in our gardens, stolen bicycles, and Arabs collecting herbs.

Now, I suppose in the wake of the riots of 2000, all of the communities in our area are being equipped with massive steel entrance gates that roll on tracks, opening and closing ponderously in response to a signal from a remote control or a cell phone. People who complain about the inconvenience are assured that the gate will only be kept closed from midnight to 5 A.M.—and that there will still be a guard on duty from midnight to 5 A.M. (The quaint custom of rotating overnight guard duty among ourselves disappeared with privatization: It's hard to explain to your employer that you came late to work because you were up all night guarding the gate.) I gather that the gate is not really meant to keep out wandering cows, teenage bicycle thieves, or herb gatherers, but rather, is being put in place "just in case" we are attacked, besieged by . . . by whom? Mobs of urban proletarians hungry for bread? Bloodthirsty Arabs seeking to drive us into the sea?

Some people love the gate. It makes them feel safe, protected, fortified. It confirms their self-image as embattled pioneers (colonists?)

standing firm for civilization inside their stockade against the terrorists and savages at the gate.

I, on the other hand, am among the soft-minded faction who
hate the gate, for it is an unmistakable symbol of our distrust of our
neighbors, of our insecurity, of our outsiderness—and as such, I fear
it will be a self-fulfilling prophecy.

25. City and Country *(May 14, 2005)*

> Then they said, "Come, let us build us a city with a tower that
> reaches the sky, so that we can make a name for ourselves . . ."
> —Genesis 11:4

> The height reached seven miles . . . and if a worker fell and
> died they wouldn't pay attention, but if a brick fell they would
> sit and weep and say, "Who will bring us another like that
> one?"
> —*Pirkei D'Rabbi Eliezer* 24

It seems that from earliest times, there was a tendency to see the city
as a place of alienation, in which human caring is overwhelmed by
the needs and achievements of the masses. And still, today many see
the big city as a place of crowded isolation, of anonymity. We carefully avoid eye contact on the subway; the uninvolved bystander
has become the emblem of city life. Out in the country you expect
a different kind of human fabric. It is the rural folk who live in a
rich network of mutual assistance, who look out for each other and
even sacrifice for each other in a way that city dwellers can only read
about in novels and in *Reader's Digest*. Community seems to be a
characteristic of the periphery, as individualism and alienation are
the hallmarks of urban life.

Part of the Zionist revolution against urban Jewish life was an
idealization of the rural peasant community—whether the villages

of the *muzhik* in Russia or of the *felach* in Palestine. We longed for the healthy, organic community, where we would help each other battle the elements and make the land—and ourselves—productive and strong, tranquil, and happy. And so we founded a number of different models of rural communities, each representing a different level of communal obligation and sharing; each was and is an attempt to create a viable community, with just the right mix of intimacy and individualism, mutual support and independence.

For a hundred years now, since the beginning of the Zionist endeavor, there have been two opposing streams of traffic in Israel—from the city to the village, from urban alienation toward the idyllic rural community—and from the suffocation and conformity perceived by many in the small rural community toward the urban centers with their promise of unlimited opportunity for self-actualization. This dilemma is illustrated nicely by a conversation I had recently with a young Arab English teacher in a nearby village. She told me her family was moving to an apartment in Acre, where she was very worried about the environment for her children—crime, drugs, violence—life in a somewhat depressed urban environment. So I asked her why she was moving. The answer: because they live in her husband's village with his extended family all around, and she feels she is being suffocated by the small town pettiness and family demands.

A short time later I met a community activist in the tiny town of Mitzpeh Ramon in the heart of the desert, who had given up her life and her business in the center of trendy Tel Aviv to bring her family to the epitome of isolated small town life—and who was thriving in her new setting. The grass is always greener . . .

Strolling through a long-established kibbutz—or an Arab village—at dusk on a summer evening, the atmosphere is seductive. A Norman Rockwell romanticism suffuses the small community—the families relaxing on the lawn or drinking coffee on the porch; a sense of tranquility and completeness, of all the residents comfortably knowing just who they are and where they belong. You want to walk into the painting. But the romance camouflages the social pressures for conformity, the power struggles, the feeling of having no privacy, no secrets, and no freedom to be who you want to be and to belong where you want to belong.

And so, our cities are full of refugees from the country—and our rural communities full of refugees from the city—as we seek the elusive balance between being whole unto ourselves and being part of the whole.

PART IV

Jewish State,
Jewish People

26. Oedipus and Orthodoxy *(August 20, 2006)*

For Torah shall come forth out of Zion, and the word of the Lord from Jerusalem . . .

—Isaiah 2:3

Zionism began a new era, not only for the purpose of making an end to the Diaspora but also in order to establish a new definition of Jewish identity—a *secular definition*. I am certain that the builders of our land will in the future sacrifice themselves for national forms, for land and language, as our ancestors accepted martyrdom for the sake of the religious content of Judaism.

—Jacob Klatzkin, *Boundaries* (1914)

It turned out that there was no consensus among the builders of the new Jewish state regarding the nature of its Jewishness. Among the assorted conceptions that were part of various wings of the Zionist movement were the following:

- A total negation of the Jewish tradition as an artifact of the exilic experience that was about to become obsolete. An extreme version of this view was that of the Canaanite Movement of the 1950s, which argued that Israeli Jews have more in common with Israeli Arabs than with Diaspora Jews, as identity is determined by the place in which you live and its culture. Interestingly, in America, there is an assumption that while the state must be neutral, individuals are expected and encouraged to be religious ("In God we trust"). The European secularism that entered Israeli culture, on the other hand, sees all religion ("the opiate of the masses") as the enemy of progress and enlightenment and humane values.

- The belief that creating a state was an act of sinful hubris and a denial of God's will and God's plan. This is the root of today's non-Zionist or anti-Zionist ultra-Orthodox positions.
- The belief that the state is indeed the fulfillment of God's messianic plan, "the first flowering of our redemption." This is the view of religious Zionism.
- The expectation, held by a small group of Reform, Conservative, and Reconstructionist leaders in the prestate years, that out of the experience of reestablishing sovereignty would arise a modernized, revitalized, and renewed Judaism.
- The view, now representative of the mainstream position of Israeli culture, that the main elements of Jewish tradition could be secularized and made into national culture, without religious belief: language, music, foods, holidays, folk literature, and the like.

The trouble was that virtually all the Zionist cultural revolutionaries who sought to discard or at least secularize Jewish tradition had received their education in Orthodox communities, so Orthodoxy was the only Judaism they knew, and they saw the institutions of the Orthodox community (whether they loved or hated them) as the repositories of the tradition, keepers of the flame, the authentic source. Thus, even while they were rebelling against Orthodoxy, it exerted upon them a pull, an authority, a sense of being the real thing, the genuine article. There was a sense that while we cultural pioneers may reject Orthodox belief and lifestyle, we need to keep the Orthodox around to keep us grounded—to keep the tradition alive for whenever we may need to refer to it, to adapt parts of it, to satisfy our nostalgia for it. And so we developed an ambivalent ideology of hating our Orthodox "father," but still loving him, rejecting him and his authority, but being unable to separate from him, fearing that if he were really to disappear, we would remain rootless, cut off, our identity somehow crippled.

Thus, it seems to me that the cover story we tell ourselves, that the Orthodox influence on Israeli society is simply a result of cynical manipulation of coalition politics (none of the big parties can get a majority, so to form a ruling coalition they need the Orthodox parties, whose price for joining is maintenance of Orthodox control of certain budgets and of certain legal areas, like marital law) is an oversimplification. I believe that there is a deep feeling in mainstream secular Israeli society that we dare not cut loose from Orthodoxy, for to do so would be to cast ourselves adrift with no Jewish moorings, and then our very Jewish identity would be in doubt—and with it, the moral justification for Zionism itself.

The question is, Where do we go from here? Can Israeli society mature past this phase? How can we shape a Jewish society that is rooted yet open, authentic yet allowing for autonomy? For a long time it seemed that Israeli society was stuck in this ambivalence. However, the assassination of Yitzchak Rabin in 1995 seems to have been a turning point. The fact that the assassin came out of the Orthodox community caused many non-Orthodox Israelis to rethink their attitude toward tradition, seeking to reclaim it from the custodians who, it turned out, had not always been responsible guardians. The past decade has seen an interesting and hopeful flowering of the liberal movements and of nonmovement experiments in study and even in worship. So maybe we are finally growing up, Jewishly.

27. Two Wagons on a Narrow Bridge
(September 10, 2006)

Rabbi Abraham Isaiah Karelitz (1878–1953) was born in Lithuania and made *aliyah* in 1933. He held no official position and belonged to no political movement. But his modest personality and his creative halachic rulings made him a widely respected and consulted leader. Like many rabbis, he was known by the name of his major (or, in his case, his first) book, a halachic treatise called *Chazon Ish, Vision of Man*. Rabbi Karelitz is famously reported to have said to Ben Gurion: "When two wagons meet head-on on a narrow path, the empty one must yield the right of way to the one that is heavily laden." This metaphor is supposed to describe the encounter between the religiously observant community and the nonobservant majority in Israel—and we often apply it, without thinking about it, to decisions of religious policy in many contexts, including Diaspora ones. Needless to say, the image is offensive to non-Orthodox Jews. Why must we be compared to an empty wagon? Why should we be considered less complete, less spiritually "laden" than any other type of Jew? Why are we any less deserving of respect, of the right-of-way, than a person who happens to have a different view of the authority of halachah? And more disturbing: Why do we ourselves, consciously or subconsciously, accept this distinction? Why are so many Reform Jews supporters of movements and institutions that deny our own authenticity? How is it that we, ourselves, seem to accept that the Orthodox are indeed the "keepers of the flame," the drivers of heavily laden carts—implying that our own carts are empty and less worthy?

The sympathetic interpretation of Rabbi Karelitz's comparison is that since the Orthodox consider adherence to the system of mitzvot compulsory—they have no freedom to compromise—while the nonobservant think the mitzvot don't really matter, those who don't really care should yield to those who care very much. Therefore, for example, the Israeli army maintains only kosher kitchens, based on the assumption that those who don't keep kosher can always eat kosher food without having to compromise their principles, while those who keep kosher don't have the option of eating nonkosher food. This principle governs many areas of public life in Israel and in many Diaspora communities (e.g., communal Jewish schools in North America, even if most of their students are not *shomrei Shabbat*, don't take school trips on Shabbat).

The unsympathetic interpretation, of course, is that the image of the wagons implies that non-Orthodox Jews are lacking in principles and/or knowledge and/or commitment. This makes us angry, as we believe that our knowledge of and commitment to freedom, humane values, a historically conscious relationship to the Jewish tradition, spirituality, social justice—these make our wagons very heavy indeed, perhaps even heavier than the load of ritual mitzvot that weigh down our Orthodox fellow travelers. And, if so, why are we the ones who always have to give way?

Perhaps the solution (to the extent that there can be one) is not in weighing the wagons, but in widening the road, so there is room for both. What we need is not a set of more complicated traffic laws, but more courteous drivers, who are sensitive to the needs of others on the road. Thus, while even zealous secularists may have to serve in a Spam-less army (!), by the same token those who are deeply committed to Shabbat may have to accept a Jewish state in which those who want to can go to the movies on Friday night. Finding such compromises may sound easy, but implementing them can be tricky. For example, if there is to be public transportation available for those who want it on Shabbat, how can we ensure that Orthodox would-be bus drivers do not suffer discrimination for their refusal to be available to work seven days a week?

I think it is easier to praise pluralism than to implement it in real life. It seems that our individual freedoms do not exist in a vacuum, but impinge on those of other people. Building a society that balances conflicting commitments and freedoms—and the need for common denominators—is a messy process, involving politics and religion, power and principles. It has been a central challenge of Zionism for over a century, and it doesn't look like we are going to solve the problem any time soon.

28. Stereotypes and Hypocrisy *(October 1, 2006)*

> Will you steal and murder and commit adultery and swear falsely, and sacrifice to Baal, and follow other gods whom you have not experienced, and then come and stand before Me in this house which bears My name and say, "We are safe"?
> —Jeremiah 7:9–10

This year, as part of a larger event at our seminar center, a number of people signed up for a workshop to explore possibilities for those who define themselves as secularists to find meaning in the High Holy Days. Rosh HaShanah and Yom Kippur, being synagogue-based without many home or public rituals or symbols, have been the most resistant to transformation to secular cultural celebrations. Thus, many Israelis who feel estranged from the synagogue have trouble finding a meaningful way to observe these holidays.

Not surprisingly, in the discussion of repentance and introspection, a comment was made that the problem with the Orthodox is that they are obsessed with ritual technicalities but don't seem to care about moral behavior. This is a common sentiment among non-Orthodox Jews of all types, and one that the popular media do everything they can to reinforce. Of course, the tension—between the "easy" path of acting as though ritual is the most important thing, and the more difficult challenge of living a life of righteousness and mercy—has been a part of Jewish experience from ancient times; it was a major theme in the teaching of the biblical prophets. And we can all cite examples of ostensibly very observant people who have done very nasty things. However, there is something self-serving and self-righteous—and, it seems to me, unfair—in the glib assertion that the Orthodox, and especially the ultra-Orthodox, are somehow less moral than the rest of us, that hypocrisy is somehow built into the halachic system. Given the centrality of morality in halachah, and the time-honored and well-developed institutions of social welfare in the Orthodox community, it seems odd that so many Jews have adopted the anti-Semitic stereotype of ultra-Orthodox Jews as mean-spirited and dishonest. I think that this perception has several roots in the modern social reality of the Jewish world.

- It is, after all, possible to find examples of ultra-Orthodox Jews (and of Reform and Conservative and Reconstructionist and secular Jews) who *are* mean-spirited and dishonest. The traditional concept of *chilul HaShem* (profanation of God's name) refers to the reality that the public sin of one Jew brings shame not only on the community, but on the whole religion. When you're a minority, people extrapolate from the behavior of one to the image of the whole group.

- There are some norms in the Orthodox world that to us who are outside it seem wrong—for example, in the area of the status of women, or of homosexuals, or of non-Jews. The question is, Is every person who lives within the Orthodox community ipso facto an immoral person?

- Non-Orthodox Jews feel that the ultra-Orthodox perceive us as inauthentic, incomplete, even sinning Jews, and that makes us angry. And, in fact, often they really do see us that way. They also see us as ignorant of our own tradition. And, in fact, often we are.

- Orthodox Jews live in a community with a clear authority structure—and that goes against our deeply rooted commitment to individual freedom, so we see *them* as inauthentic and incomplete.

- Orthodox Jews live in a relatively closed society, to which we are outsiders, strangers, who don't understand their norms, who are not conversant with their culture, who feel out of place and uncomfortable when we find ourselves surrounded by them.

In 1947, the famous so-called status quo agreement was made, between the socialist Zionist leadership (Ben Gurion) and the Orthodox parties. It specified that the various compromises in effect at that point would be preserved in the future state. Both sides were willing to compromise, apparently out of the belief that the deal would be temporary: Ben Gurion believed that the ultra-Orthodox would disappear within a few generations, modernized out of existence. The ultra-Orthodox believed that the secular Zionists would disappear within a few generations, seeing the light and returning to the faith. And now, here we are a few generations later, stuck with each other. For both populations the challenge now is how to find a place in our vision of the Jewish state and the Jewish people, and in our own hearts, for the Other.

As in our conflict with the Arabs, so with the non-Orthodox Jews' conflict with the Orthodox: As long as each is sure they are victims and the burden of change is on the other, nothing will change. The first step toward progress, it seems to me, is for those of us who do not share the Orthodox worldview to take responsibility for our own ignorance and prejudice, becoming more knowledgable of our tradition, more secure in our knowledge, and therefore less threatened by the views of those who claim a monopoly on the true interpretation of that tradition.

29. Reforming Israel *(November 18, 2007)*

The revival of Israel will bring with it the revival of the religion. And the religion, in its revival, will cast off its old shell, that no longer fits it. . . . The religion of Israel has never ceased to be capable of development.

—Shlomo Schiller, *Zionism and Religion*

One of the most frequently requested programs at our seminar center is a lecture/workshop on "the streams of Judaism." This is particularly in demand for groups planning missions and exchange programs to North America. Just last week I did two of them—one for teenagers, the other for a group of school principals. The agenda implied by the title is not, of course, a review of the many ideological and religious divisions that have characterized our entire history (Judah and Israel, zealots and Hellenizers, Sadducees and Pharisees, Karaites and Rabbanites, Chasidim and *Mitnagdim*, etc.). The purpose is rather to give the participants a crash course in the main denominations of North American Judaism, so they won't be totally shocked upon their arrival. For all the recent growth of the liberal movements in Israel, they are still quite foreign to most Israelis.

A one-session class that covers the topic is, of course, superficial. But as the Israeli slang expression goes, "That's what there is." If I talk fast, I can do a historical survey of the development of the movements since 1800, summarize their basic ideological and cultural differences, and even have time to discuss some case studies of how the different movements have responded to specific challenges (women's rights, assimilation, homosexuality, Zionism). I find people extremely interested. Many of those from Orthodox backgrounds have trouble accepting the approaches of the liberal movements. Many of those who define themselves as part of the secular majority, when pressed, actually come to the conclusion that not only is Reform Judaism not the weird assimilationist cult they thought it was, but that it actually describes them: They identify strongly as Jews; they reject the authority of halachah; they choose from among the resources of the tradition those practices that give spirit and meaning to their lives—be it *Kiddush* on Friday night or holiday observances, even daily prayer or the dietary laws. And while many, if you ask, will tell you that their personal morality stems not from their Jewishness but simply from their humanness, at the same time they will acknowledge that they do expect Israel, as a Jewish state, somehow to manifest Jewish moral values.

When you look closely, the secular-religious divide turns out to be somewhat of a false construct. The Jewish population of Israel is highly variegated in terms of religious belief and practice, with a broad spectrum of idiosyncratic patterns of observance that don't fit any neat definition.

In the 1920s and '30s there was a circle of educators and community leaders in Jerusalem, many but not all of them from English-speaking countries and affiliated with the liberal movements, among them Henrietta Szold, Alexander Dushkin, S. D. Goitein, and Ernst Simon, who agreed with their colleague, the educator Shlomo Schiller, quoted above: In reviving Jewish national independence, we would revive the Jewish religion. The experience of applying Judaism to the realities of sovereignty, the authority of having a world center, and the possibilities of cultural creativity in a thoroughly Jewish society— taken together, these would give rise to a new, modernized, unified, revitalized Judaism. There would be mutually beneficial influences between the state and the religion. We would throw off the encrustations of exile but we would not throw away Judaism itself, as the radical secular Zionists imagined. Rather, the experience of statehood would set the religion back on its feet, vital and looking forward and ready to respond actively and flexibly to the future.

In the light of the religious strife and extremism that seem to characterize Israeli life, it is easy to dismiss those optimistic dreamers as just that. But I think that would be a mistake. Israel's vision of itself—and of the place of Judaism in the state—is far from fully articulated. It is a work in progress, not a fait accompli. The challenge is to remain sensitive to what is developing on the ground, to remain open to new forms and syntheses, not to get stuck in ortho-doxies of any kind—even Reform ones.

> I will pour out My spirit on all flesh;
> Your sons and daughters shall prophesy;
> Your old men shall dream dreams,
> And your young men shall see visions.
>
> —Joel 3:1

30. Pigs *(June 20, 2004)*

In 1956, the Knesset enacted a law empowering municipalities to pro-hibit the sale of pork. Some did so. Some enforced their prohibitions. While the vast majority of stores in Jewish communities sell only ko-sher meat, it has always been possible to get "white steak" in certain restaurants, mainly in cities like Tel Aviv, Haifa, and Eilat. In 1970, I was working as a research assistant in the Physiology Department of the Negev Institute for Arid Zone Research in Beersheba, and we made a house call to take blood samples from pigs at nearby Kibbutz Lahav; it seems that the residents of Lahav got permission to raise pigs by declaring their kibbutz a scientific research facility—and, indeed, they kept a biologist on staff and published papers on pig physiology, in order to be able to legally operate their pig farm.

This issue has come to the fore lately as the large influx of im-migrants from the former Soviet Union in the past twenty years has had a significant impact on cultural norms. Most of these im-migrants are not committed to the dietary laws—and are quite committed to the foods of their old country. Thus, grocery stores have sprung up in many neighborhoods catering to their tastes—not only smoked fish, vodka, and black bread, but a variety of pork products as well.

Recently, the Supreme Court unanimously overturned several cities' pork bans, and required them to submit revised laws that would take account of neighborhoods' religious makeup: In neighborhoods where religious Jews are a small minority, pork sale would be permitted; where there is a significant observant population, municipalities could ban it. In other words, the prohibition of pork would be a response to local public sensitivity; that is, avoiding offending the sensibilities of kashrut-observing Jews—sparing them the anguish of seeing pork, or of seeing other Jews buying it. This envisions the "problem" of pork sale as a personal one: Kashrut-observing Jews should have the right to be spared the sight, smell, and presence of pork, just as the moderate majority should have the right to be spared the sight of hard-core pornography on billboards.

However, many Israelis—Orthodox and not—see the pork question differently. For example, Rabbi Yuval Cherlow, a well-known liberal Zionist-Orthodox educator, wrote in response to the Supreme Court decision:

> Slowly, the State of Israel is shedding its collective Jewish identity. The State of Israel itself is liable to undergo a process of assimilation, one which is led by the Supreme Court and its discourse about rights. . . . The exclusive adoption of discourse about rights, in the absence of a principle which obligates the preservation of the state's Jewish identity, detracts from the state's public-Jewish character. Public solidarity disappears, as do mutual help, commitments to social morality, and open-hearted Jewish ethos. (Yuval Cherlow, "What Does Pork Have to Do with the Supreme Court?" Haaretz.com [Hebrew], June 16, 2004)

That is, pork should not be banned because it offends the religious, but because allowing pork to be sold undermines the Jewish identity of the state. And when Jewish identity withers, so will

Jewish values. The question is, of course, whether that equation is valid: To what extent is kashrut a fundamental element of Jewish identity? To what extent is the Jewishness of the Jewish state manifest in how difficult the state makes it for a citizen to obtain a BLT? While only about 15–25 percent of Israelis could be defined as Orthodox, a recent survey shows that 58 percent refrain from eating pork. That means that for most of the population, pork does have symbolic significance as an element of their Jewish identity. However, are Jewish values served by preventing the other 42 percent from eating pork? Or at least by making it inconvenient for them to do so?

I must admit that I agree with Rabbi Cherlow's argument that the prohibition of pork should not be seen as based on protecting kashrut-observing Jews from the trauma of seeing pork; after all, the halachah does not prohibit seeing or even petting pigs (dogs, cats, horses, donkeys, and camels aren't kosher, either)! However, once we let the genie of democracy and individual rights out of the bottle, I'm not sure we can stuff it back inside. There are all kinds of Jews, and many of them see no conflict between their Jewishness and their consumption of pork. Eating pork is certainly a victimless crime (except for the pig). No one has suggested that Christians in Israel be prohibited from raising pigs and eating pork. So, can a democratic state really prohibit some of its citizens from buying certain foods? And can a Jewish state ignore the significance of the abstention from pork (even to the point of martyrdom) as a symbol of Jewish identity?

31. *Shabbes!* *(June 27, 2004)*

The laws of the Shabbat . . . are like mountains suspended by a hair, a large number of laws based on only a few biblical verses.
　　　　　　　　　　　　　　　　　　　—*Mishnah Hagigah* 1:8

More than Israel has kept [observed] the Shabbat, the Shabbat
has kept [preserved] Israel.

—Achad Ha'am, *Shabbat and Zionism*

Before we made *aliyah,* my wife and I lived in a pluralistic Jewish community in Philadelphia, and our kids went to a Solomon
Schechter day school. Jews were a minority in our neighborhood,
but Friday night for our community had certain expectations and
a certain spirit that came naturally. It was not a night for going out,
unless it was to another family for Shabbat dinner. Then we came
to the Jewish state, where, if you don't attend an Orthodox school,
all class parties are on Friday nights. Be there or be square. Then
the kids got their driver's licenses, and we noticed that as midnight
approached on Friday and we were getting ready for bed, they were
getting dressed to go out. "Where are you going?" "To ___ club/
pub." "But it's Friday night; nothing is open tonight." "Right, Mom/
Dad. See you in the morning." Amazing how many times we had
the same conversation before we got it.

Like so many Diaspora Jews, we had a hard time relinquishing
our myths about a Jewish state. While we knew objectively that most
Israeli Jews define their Jewishness as national or cultural, and not
religious, still, we clung to the notion that in a Jewish state, Shabbat
must be special. Coming to live here was supposed to make observing traditions like Shabbat easier, not harder; wasn't the Jewish environment what Israel was supposed to be about? No Christmas carols
in public school—and no basketball games on Friday night.

Not so simple! Under the British Mandate, no nationwide laws
could be enacted specifying Shabbat observance, but municipalities
could enact local ordinances. In mixed cities, none were enacted—
but in places with overwhelmingly Jewish populations, like Tel Aviv,
city law could force businesses to stay closed on Shabbat. When the
state was declared, the coalition agreed to take over the status quo
with respect to religious law; thus, to this day, public buses do not

run in Tel Aviv—but they do in Haifa, which was and is a mixed city. And there is now a body of national legislation regarding Shabbat, too. For example, El Al may not operate on Shabbat—nor may trains or interurban buses. Special permits are needed for agencies and services like the electric company and the police force to do necessary work on Shabbat. Violations of these restrictions have caused coalition crises more than once over the years. When Tel Aviv does enforce Shabbat closings, the municipal inspectors giving out the fines are Arabs—who, of course, are permitted to work on Shabbat.

On the other hand, most Israelis do not observe most Shabbat prohibitions, and are happy to travel, shop, and be entertained on Friday night and Saturday. There are two common patterns: Those who go to bed early and get up early to spend all day Saturday on an excursion—a hike, a day at the beach, a picnic in a national park, a bike trek, and the like; and those who go out to a club or party after midnight, get home at 6:00 A.M. and sleep most of the day. And in the past few years, a number of large suburban shopping malls have opened on Shabbat, offering a new form of Shabbat entertainment.

It may be hard for North Americans to understand the intensity of the Shabbat conflict because they have Sunday, which makes observing Shabbat a lot easier: If you have a two-day weekend, on both days of which stores and places of entertainment are open, then it's easy to set aside Shabbat and do all the shopping and errands on Sunday. In Israel, for decades, Shabbat was the whole weekend: Businesses and schools operated Sunday through Friday, so if you refrained from, say, yard work or family excursions or shopping on Shabbat, it was very difficult to find a time to do these things. In the past twenty years or so more and more offices—and now schools, too—have begun to close on Friday. While it's not the same as Sunday, it's a lot better than nothing, and the two-day weekend is becoming more and more of a cultural norm. Obviously, it doesn't help if you work in retail. . . .

My own leanings are certainly opposed to religious coercion, but the more Shabbat business and culture there is, the more jobs there are in the Jewish state for which observant Jews need not apply and the more cultural activities there are which *shomrei Shabbat* may not enjoy, which seems a strange irony. And if, in the Jewish state, Shabbat—perhaps the central symbol of Jewish identity since ancient times—succumbs to materialism and globalization and the sanctity of individual rights, then it seems not wholly out of place to ask, "OK, so what *is* Jewish about this state, anyway?"

32. The Cyprus Solution *(July 4, 2004)*

He (the priest) may marry only a woman who is a virgin. A widow, or a divorced woman, or one who is degraded by harlotry—such he may not marry.

—Leviticus 21:13–14

For most Israeli Jews, even those who define themselves as non-observant, kashrut and Shabbat still have symbolic meaning. Like many non-Orthodox Jews in America, here, too, there are lots of people who observe some kind of kashrut, who recognize Shabbat through at least some of its traditions, even as they reject the authority of any rabbinical establishment to tell them what they must do or not do. And while there are certainly those who are militantly *anti-,* there are probably more who, while themselves nonobservant, respect and even admire those who are consistent in their personal adherence to these two central pillars of traditional Jewish life.

With all the controversy around them, kashrut and Shabbat are easy; they carry a symbolic weight that transcends their halachic details. But there are other areas of halachah that, while they may be of equal significance to the Orthodox community, are seen in a wholly different light by the nonobservant majority. The marital restrictions in the above biblical passages, for example, are still valid in the eyes of halachah and affect people's lives. Unlike kashrut and Shabbat, however, the only symbolism these practices carry for the nonobservant population is of the obsoleteness and even the inhumanity of the tradition. It can and does happen that a Jewish couple turns to the office of the rabbinate to be married, only to be told that they may not marry, as the man is a cohen and the woman a divorcée. Volumes have been written giving the rational, psychological, historical, spiritual, and even medical justifications for observing Shabbat and kashrut today. Any attempt to do the same for these marital restrictions would result in a thin pamphlet indeed.

In the United States, if the couple belong to an Orthodox community, then presumably they will accept the decree; if not, they can turn to a non-Orthodox rabbi or have a civil ceremony. Here, however, they have no options at all, as marriage in Israel is defined as a religious practice, and therefore may only be performed by a recognized religious authority—there is no civil marriage. And since the government recognizes only the chief rabbi as the final arbiter of Jewish law—and he does not recognize the authority of Reform and Conservative rabbis—all Jewish marriages must be performed by Orthodox rabbis. Thus, in the Jewish state, there is no way for a cohen to marry a divorcée, or a Jew to marry a non-Jew, or for the child of a second marriage to get married himself if his mother's first marriage was dissolved without an Orthodox divorce.

But wait, there's more: A civil or other non-Orthodox ceremony that occurs in a place where such things are legal is accepted as a binding marriage under Jewish law and by the state. Therefore, if the cohen and his divorced fiancée have a civil ceremony in, say, Cyprus, then upon their return to Israel they are a fully "kosher" married couple. And since Cyprus, a popular resort destination, is only a one-hour flight away, travel agents have seen the light, and

offer honeymoon packages that include the wedding ceremony itself, with all necessary paperwork. Clearly, the Palestinians have a
potential gold mine here. . . .

It is in the area of marital law that the entanglement of religion
and state in Israel causes actual suffering, and is most blatantly in
conflict with the norms of individual freedom that are central to
modern democracies. The growth of the liberal movements in Israel
is due in large part to this dissonance—and to the corresponding
desire of increasing numbers of couples to circumvent the rabbinical marital restrictions. I believe that, ultimately, the system will
collapse, and no coalition agreement will be enough to prevent the
disengagement of the state from the Orthodox rabbinate with respect to marital law.

33. Joining the Club *(June 4, 2006)*

> Where you go I will go, and where you lodge I will lodge; your
> people shall be my people, and your God my God; where you
> die I will die, and there I will be buried.
>
> —Ruth 1:16–17

The Scroll of Ruth is traditionally read in the synagogue before the
Torah reading on the morning of Shavuot. This beautiful, gentle
story weaves together a human, family drama, a description of the
agricultural life of ancient Israel, laws of the Torah, and the larger historical picture (King David was a great-grandson of Ruth and Boaz).
Reading this *M'gilah* on Shavuot helps restore some of the "Israel
context" of the holiday. After all, the Torah was given in the Sinai
desert, not in Israel—and today, our main association with Shavuot
is the giving of the Torah. With modernization and diasporization,
the agricultural basis of the festival has largely been forgotten. Ruth
helps return us to the original context of the day, in the beginning of

the barley harvest (1:22), when the mitzvah of leaving the corners of the field unharvested for the poor was really practiced.

Biblical texts, of course, take on greater or lesser degrees of meaning and relevance as our historical and cultural circumstances change. In every generation and every place, we read through different lenses — and hence see the characters and their behaviors differently. This year, in the Israeli daily newspaper to which we subscribe, there were three separate op-ed pieces in the *erev* Shavuot edition relating the story of Ruth to Israeli immigration policies. While each took a slightly different tack, relating to different aspects of the problem (foreign workers, Palestinian family reunification, conversion), all were based on the assumption that their readers would know the story of Ruth, that they would know of its association with the holiday, and that they would appreciate the attempt to translate the ancient narrative into a modern context.

So here we have Ruth, a Jew by choice, leaving behind her birth family and culture and homeland to follow her mother-in-law back to *Eretz Yisrael*. And her devotion is rewarded as she becomes the ancestor of the Davidic dynasty. The questions come thick and fast:

- Would Ruth have been allowed in under the Law of Return?
- Would the immigration police have deported her if they had caught her?
- What kind of conversion did she undergo? Reform? Orthodox?
- Or was her simple declaration of loyalty to Naomi, her people, and her religion (quoted above), sufficient?
- How did this moving biblical account of a personal connection overcoming the ethnic and religious gap morph into the halachah that mandates the repeated discouragement of prospective converts, in order to test the sincerity of their motivation to join the Jewish people?

The Zionist revolution in the nature of Jewish identity has created surprising dissonances regarding conversion. If Jewish identity is seen as secular and national, it would seem that one ought to be able to join the Jewish people by means of some kind of secular naturalization process. Yet, while many (I'm not sure it's even a majority) of nonreligious Israelis disagree with the policy that all conversion is an Orthodox religious process here, rarely does one hear any ideas for how to replace it. Indeed, it is an interesting dilemma: Should there be such a thing as nonreligious conversion to Judaism? That is, should there be a way to join the Jewish people without accepting the tenets of Jewish religion (Orthodox, Reform, or whatever)?

The issue of conversion has become particularly vexing of late with the large number of immigrants from the former Soviet Union who are not Jewish by any definition. Many of these people want to convert to Judaism; some do so; others are put off by the requirement of the Orthodox rabbinical establishment that they commit to living an Orthodox lifestyle. And others simply aren't interested, either because they just don't care about religious categories and identities—or because they are happy with their Christian or Muslim affiliation.

In the Diaspora, we have functioned for the past two centuries with multiple options for conversion, determined by particular communities and movements. And, somehow, we have managed to retain a sense of Jewish peoplehood and a common identity that transcends our ideological and theological disputes. Indeed, one of the uniting factors has been Israel. Therefore, it is ironic that in Israel, where you might expect that we'd have even more in common beyond our differences in religious belief and practice, such pluralism of approaches is not possible.

It turns out that trying to transfer rabbinical authority from the autonomous community to the centralized state has not been good for the state—or for rabbinical authority. The state cannot replace the community, and it seems to me that the very sustainability of the state depends on the restoration of the role of the community—a pluralistic variety of communities—in religious life.

34. Not What We Had in Mind *(November 30, 2008)*

> At the end of the twenty years during which Solomon con-
> structed the two buildings, the Lord's House and the royal
> palace—since King Hiram of Tyre had supplied Solomon with
> all the cedar and cypress timber and gold that he required—
> King Solomon in turn gave Hiram twenty towns in the region
> of Galilee.
>
> —I Kings 9:10–11

The ORT network of high schools in Israel (which includes dozens of schools all over the country) has been supporting a "Jewish roots" program in all of its schools, designed to encourage pluralistic Jewish study, both informal and formal. It is an impressive effort and many teachers and principals—and students—have been moved by the experience, finding personal satisfaction and empowerment in this exposure to Jewish sources in an open, non-Orthodox, nonjudgmental setting. The staff of our center have been part of the effort for the past year, providing in-service training and support for the Jewish roots teachers and coordinators in several schools in our area.

Recently, I was meeting with a group of tenth-grade homeroom teachers for our monthly in-service session to review progress and plan activities for their classes. We got into a discussion of goals, and I mentioned that, for me, a key goal was helping the students to find roots for their ethical values in Jewish texts. Several teachers raised the question of how the non-Jews in their classes would relate to that goal. That left me speechless for a while. I guess I knew, in the back of my mind, that there are non-Jews in Jewish schools here; after all, there are many immigrants from the former Soviet Union, for example, who, while Jewish for purposes of the Law of Return (one Jewish grandparent), don't actually identify as Jews—and in some cases are practicing Christians. But it turns out that here in the Galilee that's only part of the non-Jewish population. There are Arabs (Muslim, Christian, and Druze) who choose to send their children to Jewish high schools in the cities, seeking a higher academic level than they may obtain in their village schools. And there are the South Lebanese Army (SLA) kids: During Israel's presence in Lebanon from 1982 to 2000, our close ally there was the South Lebanese Army, consisting of Christians from the region (remember, Lebanon has been, from its inception, in a state of intermittent internecine strife among Sunnis, Shiites, Druze, and Christians). When Israel suddenly withdrew from Lebanon in 2000, it seemed obvious that the SLA members and their families, if left without Israeli protection, would face terrible retribution from their neighbors. Therefore, Israel granted them asylum here and a few thousand of them have settled in Jewish towns across the Galilee, seeking, ambivalently, to integrate into the Jewish culture, and sending their kids to Jewish schools. Many of them are well-educated, multilingual—Lebanon was always seen as a piece of Europe in the Middle East. They are sad here, cut off from family and culture, not at home anywhere.

Indeed, one of the teachers confided, there is a successful, cute, popular SLA kid in one of her classes, and when she sees him hugging and kissing a Jewish girl, it freaks her out. So there you have it: There is no escape from the problems of modern life for Jews, even in the Jewish state. The Jewish state never has been and never will be 100 percent Jewish—and whether we like it or not, as long as it is a democracy that recognizes individual freedom, as long as it engages in the world—in trade, in intellectual exchange, in military alliance— it will have to struggle with the same problems of open society that Jewish communities elsewhere face. Perhaps in a different dosage, perhaps with different emphases; but we cannot cut ourselves off from the "identity marketplace" that characterizes open, Western societies. If we want our children to have strong Jewish identities, if we want them to marry Jews, we can't count on the environment, on isolating them in a nominally Jewish state. Israel, of course, is a very special place, in some ways a Jewish place. But at the same time—it's just like anyplace else.

35. The Price of Statehood *(October 15, 2006)*

We support the poor of the Gentiles together with the Jewish poor, for the sake of peace.
—Rambam (Maimonides), *Mishneh Torah*,
Laws Regarding Pagans 10:5

In the wake of the Second Lebanon War, the Jewish Federation of North America demonstrated an unprecedented outpouring of philanthropic support, collecting over $300 million for the Israel Emergency Campaign. This was badly needed to help the residents of the north whose lives were disrupted by the rocket attacks: homes damaged, businesses bankrupted, tourism crushed, children traumatized, and so on. And the rebuilding is, of course, ongoing. This process raises an interesting question—one that has been around for a long time, but is thrown into sharp relief by the current situation:

Approximately 50 percent of the citizens of the north of Israel are Arabs—Muslims, Christians, and Druze. Nearly 50 percent of those killed by katyusha attacks were Arabs, as the rockets fell indiscriminately on the patchwork of communities that make up the Galilee—and the Arab communities tended to be less well equipped with shelters and sirens. As a democracy attacked by an enemy from abroad, the State of Israel is of course obligated to protect all its citizens without discrimination; and in the reconstruction after the war, it must aid all communities proportionately. Obviously, like the German-Americans in the First World War, the Japanese-Americans in the Second World War, and the Arab-Americans today, a minority with familial, ethnic, even ideological connections to the enemy is automatically in a difficult position—and places the majority in the difficult position of having to decide on the balance between the rights and protections due a citizen and the right of the state to protect itself. Nevertheless, it would be pretty hard to defend a policy of discriminating in the allocation of resources among citizens based on ethnic identity.

On the other hand, the Jews of North America are under no such obligation. They are not citizens of the Israeli democracy, and their interest, as in all Jewish philanthropy—whether it goes to Russia or Argentina or Brooklyn—is in helping fellow members of the Jewish people, out of a strong sense of family, of mutual support, of solidarity. So should the funds collected by the North American Jewish community be designated for Jews in Israel only? There are certainly strident voices in the community arguing just that.

However, it seems to me that since 1948, the traditional model of Jewish philanthropy is no longer valid in the case of Israel. Jews around the world want there to be a Jewish state that is strong and secure. World Jewry, over the past century, has poured billions of philanthropic dollars into the building and strengthening of Israel. Most of them agree that the state they envision will be a democracy, with strong civic institutions, social stability, and economic justice. They want to be proud of being associated with it and of having helped to build it. They want it to have good prospects for long-term survival.

That being the case, I believe that Jewish philanthropy to the state has to be directed to all of Israeli society, not just to the Jewish citizens. If American Jews care about the future of Israel, about its survival, they cannot treat it as just another embattled Jewish community. If they want to secure Israel's future, they cannot ignore the glaring social and economic and educational needs of the 20 percent of the citizens (50 percent in the Galilee) who are not Jewish.

It seems that there is some recognition of this by the mainstream leadership, but there is also ambivalence, especially in the face of the many donors who still embrace the traditional model.

If this were the Ukraine, we could say that our obligation is to the Jewish community, and the needs of the non-Jews are someone else's problem. But Israel is not just another Diaspora Jewish community; it is our state, responsible for all its citizens. There is no someone else.

36. Remember! *(December 3, 2006)*

> We will not forget and we will not forgive!
> —Poster seen around Israel near anniversary
> of Yitzchak Rabin's death

Who exactly are *we* and what exactly will we not forget and whom will we not forgive?

Without knowing the seasonal context—if you encountered this poster around Yom HaShoah, for example—you might assume that it referred to the Nazis and their collaborators, or to the Palestinian terrorists and their collaborators, people who committed irredeemably evil acts. We must remember these acts and their perpetrators, so as not to allow ourselves ever to lapse into a sense of forgiveness by default, for a world where such acts are forgiven becomes an evil world. We vowed to remember the Holocaust, perhaps, to save it from ever being taken for granted, made trivial, forgiven.

However, while the poster resonates with the emotional energy of the Holocaust, it is not about the Holocaust and it is not about terrorism. So what does it mean?

One possibility is that *we* are the people of the State of Israel, and that we will not forget that shocking and tragic night when Yigal Amir assassinated Yitzchak Rabin, showing us the black depths to which political polemic could descend. And we will not forgive Amir for his act. This implies, I suppose, that we are angry that the court recently permitted him conjugal rights, allowing him to marry and father a child while in his prison cell (he is serving a life term). It also implies that we think that there are some in our midst who believe that forgiveness is possible for the assassin—hence, this poster to reaffirm our rejection of that belief.

Another possibility is that *we* are the left wing of Israeli political discourse, the so-called peace camp, who feel that the bullet aimed at Rabin was aimed at all of us and all we believe in, who know that while Yigal Amir may have acted alone, his act was silently (or not so silently) encouraged and supported by various segments of the right wing of Israeli society. Thus, the poster is an ominous threat: We know who killed Rabin and shot down the peace he tried to cultivate, and we will neither forget nor forgive, and there will someday be a settling of accounts. Amir may have taken the fall, but there are thousands among us who see violence as acceptable in the service of God's will as they understand it—and who don't think Amir is beyond forgiveness.

Still another possibility is that the poster is a leftover from the struggle over the withdrawal from Gaza last summer, when such rhetoric, directed by the settlers and their supporters against those who sanctioned and carried out the evacuation, was quite common.

In other words, this simple poster is really very economical, and whoever printed it, with a little marketing savvy, should be able to sell one to just about all of us regardless of our political or ideological affiliation. It is kind of a universal expression of free-floating anger; everybody can identify with it. It rides on a powerful cultural theme that has flowed through us since the Holocaust: memory as defiance, defiant memory as identity. Our answer to those who wanted us to be forgotten—or who wanted their evil to be forgotten—is to remember, to remember, to remember. We remember with all our might—indeed, sometimes I fear that we devote so much energy to remembering past evils, grudges, insults, wounds, injustices, and victimization, that we lose sight of the future.

There may indeed be situations in which it is appropriate not to forget and not to forgive. However, I find the declaration in this poster chilling and dehumanizing—a defiant rejection, in the name of the Jewish people, of the Jewish value of the hope for redemption.

PART V

Arab and Jew

37. Toward Democracy *(December 24, 2000)*

THE STATE OF ISRAEL will be open for Jewish immigration and for the Ingathering of the Exiles; it will foster the development of the country for the benefit of all its inhabitants;
it will be based on freedom, justice and peace as envisaged
by the prophets of Israel; it will ensure complete equality of
social and political rights to all its inhabitants irrespective of
religion, race or sex.

—Israel Declaration of Independence

[*Author's Note:* At the time of the High Holy Days in 2000, riots
broke out in Arab villages and towns around Israel; it was not clear
if this was out of identification with the outbreak of violence in the
West Bank and Gaza, the Second Intifada that started then, or a general expression of frustration by the Arab citizens of Israel over the
failure of Israel to provide them with equal rights and opportunities.
Thirteen Arabs were killed by police and army gunfire. These were
the events that encouraged me to start writing *Galilee Diary*.]

Since the rioting stopped in mid-October, there has been a flurry of
meetings around the Galilee seeking to organize new initiatives in

Arab-Jewish cooperation and dialogue. I have been spending a lot of time at meetings, from the initial wave of *sukkat shalom* discussions, at which Arabs and Jews sat in a circle to speak about their feelings and their commitment to change to the current steering and planning committees, and have heard any number of ideas, everything from employment opportunity projects to regional planning to a Jewish-Arab circus. It is neither surprising nor encouraging to realize that most of the participants are people who were already involved, on some level, in similar conversations in the past. It feels good and right to me to be a part of these projects, as I feel that I was not active enough before these events, that I should have been more sensitive to the situation of the Palestinian Arabs of Israel. The situation brings back memories of the experiences of the civil rights struggle in the United States in the 1960s.

For me, after getting over some initial feelings of fear and betrayal, the rioting was a kind of wake-up slap, jolting me out of a comfortable, fairly passive complacency: For years I have been explaining to tourists the delicate fabric of coexistence in our area, how while the Arabs had legitimate grievances, they had found that the way to resolve them was to remain true to democratic processes, to "play the system." I said that, for all its imperfections, Israel is a democracy, and can be held to a democratic standard. I said that while we aren't sure just how, we believe that a Jewish state can also be a democracy, and that we have to keep working on perfecting it. I said that our treatment of the Arabs living among us will be the moral litmus test of our success. And then, standing on the front porch, looking across the valley to the Muslim Arab village of Sha'ab, a twenty-minute walk from here, whose relationship with the Jewish communities had always been seen as a model, I could hear rhythmic chanting in Arabic as brush and forest fires broke out in different spots along the ridge above the village.

And I didn't know what to think. What if the rioters marched on our community? What if everything I had been believing and saying was naive self-persuasion, as so many on the right had always claimed, and the Arabs of Israel were just biding their time before driving us into the sea? And how could I reconcile such doubts with the reality of the local Arabs I knew personally, whose commitment to democracy seemed so clear? It took a while, but a series of conversations since then has convinced me that I was both right and wrong: right that the Arabs of Israel are not committed to the destruction of Israel and the expulsion of the Jews; wrong to think that the calm status quo indicated a stable modus vivendi. What I have learned since October is that, to a large extent, we have failed the test of democracy, that I was overly complacent and somewhat ignorant to think that, despite some frustrations and limitations, we were on a clear path toward putting our democratic ideals into practice.

The reality is that we have a long way to go. We have placed the Arabs of Israel in a double bind. We expect them to act like good citizens, but at every airport security checkpoint, every job interview, every zoning hearing, we treat them as potential enemies. Then, when they respond by expressing reservations about their loyalty to Zionism, we accuse them of not being good citizens, thus justifying treating them as enemies. I am convinced that much of this is based on simple ignorance: Because of geographical and cultural and historical factors, the vast majority of Israeli Jews have never spoken to an Arab except to say, "Fill it up with high octane." And most Israeli Jews have served in the army, fighting an enemy who is, generically, an Arab.

We have a lot of work to do. And the message of the October riots is that it is urgent. I worry that all the local efforts, the dialogues and committees, are just a drop in the bucket, that a national effort is needed, led by the leaders of the nation. And yet those leaders have other priorities just now. So I continue to go to meetings and to hope that micro will somehow lead to macro. . . .

[*Afterword:* Two years after the riots, a government commission of inquiry, the Or Commission, published a detailed report on the

events. The report criticized the Arab communal leadership for encouraging, if not inciting, the riots, and the police for general incom-
petence. But the most significant conclusion was that the government
had systematically failed to uphold its own values and make good on
its promises vis-à-vis the Arab population. So while the riots were,
of course, unjustified, they were not at all inexplicable.]

38. Clear Title *(February 5, 2006)*

> When you sell property to your neighbor, or buy any from
> your neighbor, you shall not wrong one another. In buying
> from your neighbor, you shall deduct only for the number of
> years since the jubilee; and in selling to you, he shall charge
> you only for the remaining crop years. . . . But the land must
> not be sold beyond reclaim, for the land is Mine; you are but
> strangers resident with Me.
>
> —Leviticus 25:14–15, 23

For the past year, I have attended a number of meetings of a group
trying to introduce a rational public planning process into a very
fraught local political issue: The Arab city of Sachnin is seeking a
shift in its boundaries, to transfer open spaces from Misgav (which is
mostly open space dotted with small Jewish communities) to Sachnin's jurisdiction for residential development. So far, this dispute
is being played out quietly, in municipal council chambers, zoning commissions, and occasional handbills and letters to the editor.
However, the tensions over land allocation/possession/jurisdiction
in this country run deep (and go back decades), and are fraught with
emotional, social, and historical implications; lurking behind the
ongoing discussions are fresh memories of the riots of 2000 in this
area—and those of Land Day in 1976.

In 1976, a land dispute occurred in this same area over the army's closing off traditional grazing lands to use as a firing range,

and over a plan publicized by the government to increase the Jewish population of the region, inauspiciously called the plan to Judaize the Galilee. The Arab leadership called a one-day general protest strike, which turned into street riots that were put down violently. Six Arabs were killed; a monument to them stands in the center of Sachnin, not far from another, newer one, for the young people killed in the riots of 2000. Since then, March 30 has been observed as Land Day.

When the Zionist settlers began to arrive in the late nineteenth century, they found a poor province of the Ottoman Empire. The Palestinian peasants lived a premodern agrarian life, using traditional farming methods, living in small villages, each ruled by a hereditary *mukhtar* (chief), in a more or less constant state of tension with the inefficient and often corrupt Ottoman bureaucracy. Although the Ottomans had instituted a system of land registration in 1858, it had not been widely accepted or consistently or fairly enforced, so that some registered titles had been unfairly usurped by village leaders and much land remained unregistered, with the local peasants relying on traditions of possession by cultivation, verbal agreements, and unrestricted grazing on the mountains on land that was technically not privately owned, but state property. By the time the Ottoman Empire collapsed in the First World War, the title to large tracts of cultivable land had been accumulated by wealthy landowners who lived in Beirut or other distant cities, and the peasants had become sharecroppers. The map of village jurisdictions was not formal; one tradition had it that the jurisdiction of a village chief reached as far as the sound of the muezzin of the local mosque could be heard.

The British, who took over after the First World War, tried to systematize land ownership and enforce registration laws, and succeeded to some extent—though it may well be that in the process they simply mapped and certified many claims of ownership that were questionable in the first place.

Meanwhile, Zionist settlers came along and, wanting to operate "by the book," purchased land, fair and square. The Jewish National Fund bought agricultural land (and even swampland), often at inflated prices, from landowning families. The problem was, of course, that the land came with its tenants, the Palestinian farmers, who did not fit into the Zionist vision of self-reliant self-redemption, achieved by cultivating the soil with our own hands. Thus, the Jews legally purchased the peasants' land—but were not interested in their continuing to rent it—nor were they willing to take on the role (which some settlers of the First Aliyah in the 1880s had been) of plantation owners employing them—anathema to kibbutzniks (then). And so it happened that on account of fidelity to ideals and not wanting to be seen as—or to see themselves as—oppressors, Jews went to great lengths to buy the land properly and to work it with their own hands. The sadly ironic result was that these same people were perceived as oppressors who pushed the peasants from their traditional holdings and didn't even offer them jobs in return. So while the activity of these immigrants certainly spurred the economy and did create increased prosperity and opportunity overall, the image of "stealers of the Palestinians' land" had been formed, and it haunts us still.

[*Afterword:* Since 2007, Israel has witnessed an extended public controversy over whether land purchased by the Jewish National Fund, now being used for building new communities and subdivisions, can rightly be restricted to "Jews only," as it was bought by the Jewish people. Are such restrictions still relevant and moral in a sovereign, democratic, Jewish state?]

39. Land and Memory *(March 12, 2006)*

While Jeremiah was in prison in Jerusalem (chapter 32) for having prophesied that the Babylonians would be victorious, the "word of the Lord" came to him and ordered him to buy a plot of land from his cousin, in the village of Anathoth, north of Jerusalem. And sure enough, his cousin came to the prison, saying, "Please, buy my land in Anathoth, in the territory of Benjamin; for the right of succession is yours, and you have the duty of redemption. Buy it." And so he did, even though he was certain that the Kingdom of Judah was about to go under any day. Which, indeed, it did.

Jeremiah's purchase was ordered by God in order to symbolize the hope of redemption, even though the country was about to be conquered by a foreign power, and chaos and suffering and exile would result. The promise of the Land of Israel as the people's eternal inheritance meant that, ultimately, the foreign conqueror would leave, and the original owners — or their heirs — would return to their birthright. This episode in Jeremiah's life casts in sharp relief the interesting interplay between private ownership and public jurisdiction. Jeremiah assumes that his private deed will remain binding through the Babylonian rule and into the restoration of Jewish sovereignty at an unknown future time. Even if the Babylonians expropriate the land and assign it to someone else, with the restoration the plot will be returned to Jeremiah or his descendants.

And now there is a Jewish government again. Alas, Jeremiah's deed has been lost, but over 90 percent of the land belongs to the state, and Jeremiah's plot can be leased for a biblical forty-nine years by his descendants. Now, ironically, it is the Palestinian Arabs who are playing the role of Jeremiah. Many of the refugees of 1948 — both internal (living in Israel but not on the land they lived on before the state was established) and external (in refugee camps or elsewhere in the world) will happily show you the key to their pre-1948 house, now occupied by a Jewish family, or destroyed to make way for Israeli construction. They keep that key as a symbol, like Jeremiah's deed (two copies of which he had placed in an earthen jar "so that they may last a long time"), of the hope of future return. One can say, of course, that there is nothing wrong with the nostalgic longing for an idealized past, and that there is a gap between the Palestinians' rhetoric and the demands of modern reality. I know a Bedouin teacher whose entire village near the Syrian border was transferred by the army in 1951 to a village near us. He was one year old. He has a life now, a good job with the Ministry of Education, grown children with college degrees, a nice house; it is hard to conceive of him picking up and moving back to his ancestral lands, where the economy was based on subsistence farming. But if you ask him, he will tell you that he is sitting on his suitcases waiting for the return. And we could find thousands of similar examples.

For an agrarian culture, there is no question that rootedness in the land is a central value, and hence a key element in Palestinian identity. The question is, as agrarian culture becomes postagrarian, what exactly is the meaning of land and the personal connection to it? The Zionist settlers came with a vision of rerooting in the land—but today we go to museums to learn about Jewish farmers. Is the Palestinian demand for return a bluff? A product of the fact that Israel and the Arab countries have not enabled the displaced Palestinians to put down new roots anywhere else? A bargaining strategy? A refusal to let go of a significant element in their identity as their society goes through the trauma of modernization? A simple demand for justice?

And—this is the fateful question—is there an alternative to a zero-sum game? Does our claim necessarily negate theirs, and theirs negate ours? Or can there somehow be room for both of us here?

40. Local Politics *(November 9, 2003)*

> You shall appoint magistrates and officials for your tribes, in all the settlements that the Eternal your God is giving you, and they shall govern the people with due justice. You shall not judge unfairly; you shall show no partiality. . . .
>
> —Deuteronomy 16:18–19

In 1948, many Arabs fled the new State of Israel during the fighting. Just how and why they fled, and how violently they were encouraged to do so, are complex questions still being debated by historians, politicians, and educators. Needless to say, this is not a neutral research subject. In any case, many stayed here and became citizens of Israel. For the first twenty years, the Galilee was under a military governor, and the Arab citizens' movements were restricted and controlled. Infrastructure and communal governance were more or less frozen. Then, in the late '60s, the decision was made to integrate the Galilee more fully into the state, and the military governor was eliminated. Water lines, sewer lines, and roads were built, and Arab municipalities were brought into the orbit of the Interior Ministry—required to hold state-sanctioned and properly conducted elections and comply with all the standard requirements for municipal administration. Previously, the standard form of village governance was rule by the leaders of the largest (and therefore most powerful) clan. The village chief, patriarch of the largest clan, was called the *mukhtar*. In the case of Sha'ab, our neighboring village, the Faur clan was dominant, a leading family of those who stayed in 1948, and who remained in control as the population of the village was augmented by refugees from three other villages destroyed in the wake of the war.

Afu Faur had been the *mukhtar,* and it was natural for him to become the first elected mayor in the '60s. He was generally associated with the Labor Party, and followed a conciliatory policy regarding neighboring Jewish communities. Not surprisingly, municipal officials, city workers, school principals, and other prominent citizens tended to have the last name of Faur. His rule seemed pretty certain, though in the mid-1990s his opponents did manage to get him indicted for petty corruption; in the end, the charges did not stand up in court.

The tension between the traditional clan system and the way of modern meritocracy is a constant theme running through the past thirty years of Israeli Arab history. It seems that the government tended to allow or even encourage the maintenance of the clan system, for it provided malleable local leadership, easily controlled through resource distribution; thus, ideological leadership and political opposition were dampened. Meanwhile, a new generation of modernized, educated leaders has arisen, people who see the system as an anachronism and an obstacle to the development of the Arabs of Israel—as individuals and as a political community. They are seeking to bring professionalism and meritocracy into village administration, but the clan machine is not only entrenched in the power structure, but represents the positive values of tradition, respect, patriarchy, "doing things our way," as opposed to the secular, atomistic, hedonistic culture of the West. Thus, what many people see as the key to personal and communal advancement is seen by others as a threat to their identity and continuity.

Sometimes the modernizers get the upper hand, only to discover a term or two later that they are the electoral victims of traditional backlash. For example, in Kaukab, another village in our area, the mayor did wonders in developing his village in terms of commerce and quality of life—yet was voted out of office because of his policy of hiring according to objective qualifications instead of by family name. On the other hand, sometimes even a traditionalist village like Sha'ab gets fed up with the high-handedness of the leading clan. Sometimes, the competing clan uses the claim of modernization simply as a guise to unseat its rivals. On the one hand, this is a local, particular issue, and every village has its own unique story. On the other hand, it seems to me that this struggle in Sha'ab and many other villages is a microcosm of the global conflicts that drive most of our headlines these days.

41. Local Drama *(July 29, 2007)*

The blood-avenger himself shall put the murderer to death; it is he who shall put him to death upon encounter.

—Numbers 35:19

We are eating a lot of stuffed grape leaves this week. It's a long story. Six years ago, when we still operated a restaurant in Shorashim, our assistant cook for about a year was a young woman from the nearby Muslim Arab village of Dir El Assad. Kamla was about thirty, the mother of two young children, petite but strong, a hard worker, and a natural cook. She left us to start a small restaurant in her village, which she gave up to open a catering business out of a commercial kitchen she and her husband installed in their home.

Two years ago a young man from the dominant Assadi clan in the village beat up a member of the Musa clan over an issue of personal insult. The perpetrator, who was apparently not a model citizen in any case, then spent two years in jail over a different matter. Three weeks ago, he had attended a wedding in the village after his release. On his way home, he was ambushed and gunned down by three of twelve brothers of the Musa clan, in front of dozens of witnesses. The murderers were arrested immediately. The next morning the loudspeakers proclaimed that the dead man would not be buried until all of the Musa brothers had left the village, which they did; the funeral was held that night, and turned into a riot, in the course of which cars and homes belonging to the banished Musas were torched.

A *sulcha* committee was formed. *Sulcha* refers to the classical process among Arab villagers of arriving at a peaceful, negotiated settlement to such clan vendettas. The committee includes community leaders, religious and otherwise, but of course has problems of built-in bias because of the clan-determined nature of the local leadership (the Assadis probably constitute half of the 10,000 residents of the village). So far, they have decreed a three-month exile of all the Musa brothers. While their wives and children are technically exempt from this ban, they have all relocated to temporary housing in other villages—their neighborhood in Dir El Assad is totally abandoned. Apparently, some kind of monetary settlement and public apology will ultimately be negotiated, unless some hotheaded young macho type messes up the process.

Kamla, it turns out, is married to one of the Musa brothers (not one of the three perpetrators). Thus, she has become somewhat of a refugee, without access to her home and kitchen, a major blow to the family's livelihood. But she has managed to organize a kitchen in her temporary accommodations, and her Jewish friends have posted a website for purchasing food, delivered by volunteers. That's why we're eating a lot of stuffed grape leaves. Also vegetarian *kubeh*.

This is not about feminism, nor is it about Islam. The gangs in Los Angeles are a lot more lethal. It is just another example (like violence against women) of the price Israel pays for cultural pluralism. In the interest of the freedom of minority groups to live according to their own cultures, Israel's political system has, to a significant extent, abdicated responsibility for defining and enforcing certain basic, common cultural and legal norms—not only among the Arabs, but among ultra-Orthodox Jews as well.

It's a tricky business, navigating the straits between premodern and postmodern; and every time we bump up against the side, someone gets hurt.

42. Separate But Equal? *(March 23, 2003)*

My father, those days, was continuously and pensively struggling with the new language that had invaded his small world and ours, imposing upon him confusion and a new type of illiteracy . . . He was learning Hebrew for beginners, as if he were . . . a new immigrant to his own country.

—Anton Shamas, "At Half-Mast—Myths, Symbols, and Rituals of the Emerging State: A Personal Testimony of an Israeli Arab," in *New Perspectives on Israeli History*, ed. L. Silberstein (1991)

The other day M., one of our Galilee Fellows whose project has been working with a teen leadership group in the neighboring village of

Sha'ab, asked me to join her for her weekly session with the group. At the previous meeting, she had presented some statistics on the disparity between Jewish and Arab citizens of Israel with respect to success on the end-of-high-school matriculation (*bagrut*) exams, and enrollment in postsecondary education. The data generated a great deal of emotion and heated debate within the group, which the kids were unable to calmly articulate to M.; hence, her invitation to me to help her try to sort it out.

There were eight teens there, all twelfth graders, the more veteran members of the larger group which numbers about twenty-five. They meet weekly with the stated purpose of practicing their spoken English. However, we know and they know that that is only part of the story, and it is the discussions of social and political questions, the contact with Jewish Israel, the opportunities to meet and host Jewish visitors from Israel and abroad that are the true substance of the project. This group seems to comprise the best and the brightest in the Sha'ab high school: smart, thoughtful, energetic, curious, and personable.

Once again, M. put the key data up on the board and a storm ensued. It seems that many of the kids insisted that the numbers couldn't be true, and were demanding to know the source. This was surprising to me, as these disparities have been public knowledge for a long time, and are among the stock-in-trade of everyone who speaks and writes on behalf of equalizing educational opportunities in Israel. To me, the numbers seem intuitively obvious and it never occurred to me to question them. It was fascinating to me to discover that instead of viewing the information as evidence of a discriminatory and unequal distribution of resources, most of the teens perceived the data as an attempt to portray the Arabs as less competent, successful, and intelligent. Instead of trumpeting the statistics as proof of their victimhood, they were ashamed by them, and wanted to find a way to disprove them.

M. led the group in an exploration of how one can interpret and argue against such data: What is the source? How can we check it? What alternative sources can we locate? Can we find local examples or counterexamples? This was a useful exercise, since a problem in this group and in Israeli public discourse in general is the lack of a culture of rational debate. We are trying to develop a style of leadership that is based not on who can shout the loudest but on who can say something worth listening to.

Meanwhile, I tried to move the conversation beyond this exercise: OK, I said, suppose the statistics are off by a factor of two, and the disparity is much smaller; let's agree that there is probably some disparity—and if so, what does it mean and what can we do about it? Again, to my surprise, there was no mention of uneven funding, facilities, teacher training, curricular materials, enrichment opportunities. Rather, they wanted to talk about the cultural issue: They said that the Hebrew/European/Western cultural bias of the *bagrut* exams and the universities puts Arabs at a disadvantage. Even though they take the exams in Arabic, the contents of the curriculum are foreign to them, not to mention the whole intellectual structure of the universities. And, of course, all university studies are conducted in Hebrew, with much of the reading, in many fields, in English.

One of the boys pointed out that at Mar Elias Academy, a highly regarded private Christian high school in a nearby village, everything is taught in Hebrew except Arabic language and literature. "Those kids score high on *bagrut* and do well in university. That's what we should have!" This set off a chaotic argument in Arabic in the group between advocates of assimilation and those who called for preserving Arabic culture no matter what the personal cost. Once we had restored order and gotten the issues clarified, agreeing that there is a difficult dilemma here and that every solution comes at a price, I wondered out loud about the possibility of an Arabic university— and the participants started shouting all over again.

For all the differences between the two situations, it is fascinating to note the parallel between the predicament of the Arabs in Israel and that of the Jews in the Diaspora: Acquiring an education that will enable a person to "make it" in the majority culture seems often to carry with it the weakening of the knowledge of and commitment to the minority's culture. In the argument among the Arab teens about going to a private Hebrew-based high school, I could hear a distinct echo of the debate in the American Jewish community over Jewish day school education.

43. Myths and Facts *(June 3, 2001)*

Thus Joshua conquered the whole country: the hill country, the Negev, the Shefelah, the slopes, with all their kings; he let none escape, but proscribed everything that breathed—as the Lord, the God of Israel, had commanded. Joshua conquered from Kadesh-barnea to Gaza, all the land of Goshen, and up to Gibeon. All those kings and their lands were conquered by Joshua at a single stroke.

—Joshua 10:40–42

An angel of the Lord came up from Gilgal to Bochim and said, "I brought you up from Egypt and I took you into the land which I had promised on oath to our fathers. And I said, 'I will never break My covenant with you. And you, for your part, must make no covenant with the inhabitants of this land; you must tear down their altars.' But you have not obeyed Me—look what you have done! Therefore, I have resolved not to drive them out before you; they shall become your oppressors . . ."

—Judges 2:1–3

The other night, I attended a lecture by Professor Ilan Pappe of Haifa University, one of the "new historians" on Jewish and Arab perspectives on the War of Independence. He and his colleagues (the most famous of whom is Benny Morris, whose *Righteous Victims* is a popular scholarly history of the rise of the state) argue that documentary evidence and interviews with witnesses indicate that the War of Independence was not exactly the way we have traditionally been taught to see it. It was not the courageous stand of a few pure Jews against the vicious multitude of Arabs—and the Arabs who fled did not all do so on their own initiative. Rather, he argues, there was a conscious and concerted effort by the Jews to get as many Arabs as possible to flee. There were massacres, there were campaigns of intimidation: The Jewish leadership understood that an ethnic Jewish state would need a clear Jewish majority to be viable, and that given the hopelessness of any kind of multicultural coexistence, and given the recent Jewish experience in Europe, the ends justified just about any means. Thus, according to this analysis, while there was certainly Arab brutality, the Arabs by no means had a monopoly on it. It was a nasty war, and terrible things were done by both sides. And therefore, it is not just anti-Semitism or mean-spiritedness that causes the Arabs of Israel to see Independence Day as a time of mourning instead of celebration (they call it the *Nakbeh,* or catastrophe). The new historians argue that the historical memory of the Arabs living in Israel has validity, and that it would be helpful for ultimate reconciliation if the Jews were to admit that the myths on which we grew up—of the Arabs' self-motivated flight, of the "purity of Jewish arms"—don't represent the whole truth.

Most of the people at the lecture, residents of the Galilee who attended the lecture in the context of their activity in Sikkuy—an organization that engages in education, research, and advocacy for equal rights—pretty much knew what to expect, and listened calmly. A few squirmed, and in the question-and-answer period argued: "But it was do or die—it was a struggle for survival. How could we have been expected to act differently?"

The man sitting next to me, however, who looked to be about fifteen years younger than the state, couldn't take it. We could see and feel his agitation, and finally he blurted out his response. "Are you trying to tell me that my father was a liar—that all of our fathers were liars? You are as bad as the Holocaust deniers! You manipulate history for your own ends! Who is to say that your version is correct? This is our land and we have a right to it. Don't you believe in the Bible? Don't you believe in the UN? They both say it is ours! What are we supposed to do, get up and go back to Europe?" Any attempts by the speaker to respond calmly only made him angrier, and after another outburst, he finally left.

He spoke, I think, for many Israelis, who are not ready to hear the story of the other, not yet able to question our sacred myths and heroes without feeling threatened and betrayed. Maybe it's a maturity thing: Little kids insist on knowing who are the good guys and who are the bad guys; as they get older, they can begin to understand that all guys are a mix of good and bad, and that there are no simple stories. Most Israelis—Jews and Arabs—are not secure enough yet to climb down from their safe, simple myths to the dangerous territory of complexity and ambiguity, and evince a willingness to consider that the other may have at least a partially valid story.

I believe that the new historians are not post-Zionists, weakening our national solidarity or our Zionist commitment; rather, I believe they are helping us to grow up, to integrate all the elements of our past, both those of which we are proud and those we would like to forget, both what was done to us and what we did to others. Sustainable Zionism is not knee-jerk patriotism, but a mature, honest, self-critical, reflective commitment to a Jewish state in the Land of Israel. Moreover, it seems to me that by studying our past honestly and openly, we don't lose the high moral ground—we gain it.

44. Names and Memory *(December 17, 2006)*

Then he said, "Let me go; dawn is breaking!" But [Jacob] said, "I will not let you go unless you bless me!" The other said to him, "What is your name?" and he said, "Jacob." "No more

shall you be called Jacob, but Israel," said the other, "for you
have struggled with God and with human beings, and you have
prevailed." Then Jacob asked, "Pray tell me now your name."
But he said, "Why do you ask my name?" And then he took his
leave of him. Jacob therefore named that place Peni'el—"For I
have seen *God face-to-face*, yet my life has been spared."

—Genesis 32:27–31

Naming, in the Bible, is a very significant act. The assigning or chang-
ing of the name of a person—often by God—is always symbolic of a
deeper understanding of identity, the essence of who that person is
or has become. Naming implies power: The naming of the animals
by Adam in Eden implies his mastery over them (Genesis 2:19–20).
Parents name their children, but children, at least in most societies,
are not allowed to address their parents by their given names. The
naming of places, too, reflects power and symbolic meanings. In the
Bible, places are often named for the memory of a significant event
that occurred there. See, for example, Genesis 21:30–32, where Beersheba is named, and Genesis 22:14, where Abraham names the site of
the binding of Isaac. If I can name a place, determine which memory
it will preserve, then I must in some way own it.

Which is why, I suppose, the issue of place names is such a sensitive one in Israel today. Recently, the mayor of Ramleh (a city near
Ben Gurion Airport, not to be confused with Ramallah, a city in
the West Bank), one of the six mixed (Arab-Jewish) cities in Israel
(the others are Lod, Jerusalem, Jaffa, Haifa, and Acre), was inter-
viewed on a national radio program; he was asked about the proposal
by some Arab city council members to restore the original Arabic
names of some of the streets in their neighborhood, the old city.
These streets had been renamed in the 1950s after various Zionist
heroes. His response was a remarkable string of unprintable exple-
tives about the Arabs and what they could do with their proposal
and themselves. This, of course, did not stop all the newspapers from
printing his words, repeatedly and with gleeful horror. A week later

a demonstration was held, calling for his removal from office by the Interior Ministry. That seems to have been, of course, the end of the matter, as we don't really do "politically correct" here—you can say the most outrageous things in public (sexist, racist, ad hominem, whatever), and there will be a brief outcry—but nothing more.

What the incident brought to the surface is an ongoing struggle over whose memories will determine the identity-geography of this land. It is often obvious that traditional Arab names of places in Israel reflect a pre-Arab memory. For example, in the cases of Zippori, Yaffo, Beersheba, and Gaza, among others, you don't have to be a scholar of Semitic languages to be able to recognize in the Arabic place name the ancient Hebrew original. There was something exciting and satisfying about finding these names waiting for the waves of *aliyah* in the late nineteenth and early twentieth centuries, preserved for Jews to reclaim. And in reclaiming and re-Hebraizing them, those making *aliyah* both proved to themselves that they really had roots here and reconnected to them. These were *our* names—so obviously this was *our* land. Almost all the Arab villages in my neighborhood of the Galilee bear the names of towns mentioned in Josephus and in the Talmudic literature, usually completely unchanged.

On the other hand, once this became our land, it became very important for us to assert our ownership and to delegitimize competing memories. Hence, street names in old Arab cities—even if they were still inhabited by Arabs—were changed to reflect modern, Zionist memories. It was natural for place names (mountains, rivers, valleys) to be Hebraized: After all, Hebrew became the language of the land. However, the assigning of Hebrew names to the communities built on the lands of villages that had been destroyed or abandoned in 1948 has been perceived by many Arabs as a deliberate ploy to erase memory and therefore culture; many of the former inhabitants of those villages still live in the area, and feel that the renaming of their villages is adding insult to injury: "OK, take our land; but do you have to take our memories, too?" From our point of view, of course, these memories are indeed threatening, and we would just as soon see them fade away. It seems, alas, that the harder one tries to repress a threatening memory, the more threatening it becomes.

45. Abraham's Children *(December 21, 2008)*

Then We gave him the good tidings of a prudent boy; and when [the boy] had reached the age of deeds with him, [Abraham] said, "My son, I see in a dream that I shall sacrifice you; consider, what do you think?" He said, "My father, do as you are commanded; you shall find me, God willing, one of the mighty of spirit."

—Qur'an, Sura 37

A recurring question among the group of imams who participated in the course on Judaism that our education center coordinated for the Interreligious Coordinating Council of Israel over the past two years was this: Why are we learning about Judaism, but we don't see Jews studying Islam? Indeed, this was an awkward question, as we did not have such an easy time collecting rabbis in the area (aside from the handful of Reform and Conservative rabbis in the Galilee and a few Orthodox rabbis known for their liberal leanings) willing to devote time on a regular basis to learning from the imams. There were several reasons for this, I think. Indeed, some rabbis simply don't feel that it is important or worthwhile to devote time and energy to learning about another religion. Some rabbis probably feel that they already have a basic knowledge of Islam from reading and from academic study, so they are not attracted to a course in basic Islam. Most of the village imams in our program were not highly educated or pedagogically sophisticated, so the prospects of serious discussion were not great. Thus, we gave up on creating a comparable course. On the other hand, it occurred to us that there might be Jewish laypersons who would be curious to encounter local imams and to learn about Islam from them. So we invited one of the participants in the course to give a class (first, just an experimental session, to see if there was interest) on Islam for Jews.

Twenty learners showed up for that first class, and many others let us know that they were interested in attending in the future. We invited Ali Aburaya, one of the imams who had been most vocal in his disappointment that the course was one-directional, and he happily agreed to present on the topic of the holiday that was about to take place (that November), Id el Adha, the Feast of the Sacrifice. He is imam of the central mosque in the town of Sachnin, and teaches Islam and physical education in the local school. He wears informal Western clothes, no special headgear—you would take him for the gym teacher that he is.

He brought in the passage from the Qur'an describing God's command to Abraham to sacrifice his son, and explained the different traditions of interpretation (was it Isaac or Ishmael?), and the traditions of the holiday commemorating the event. The class deluged him with questions on everything from textual interpretation to folk customs to the structure of Islamic law and literature. They kept on asking until he had to leave, and all agreed that a series was called for. I think he was pleased and a little surprised by the level of interest and curiosity. He was honest and open and patient, but one thing that struck many of us was the cultural gap between our way of thinking and his; this came out in one exchange with a questioner. A participant asked: In our tradition, there is extensive and intensive questioning and discussion about Abraham's act—Was it justified? Was it problematic? How could God make such a command? Then the final question: Do you have a similar discussion? Ali's answer was basically: No, there is no problem—Abraham and his son demonstrated perfect faith, and that's all there is to it. I don't know enough to know how representative this village preacher was of contemporary Islamic thought, but on the local level the cultural distance between him and us was clear. Nevertheless, we plan to meet again next week.

As I write this, "Ignorant armies clash by night," while ignorant civilians are trying, quietly, to create some light.

46. Listening *(January 11, 2009)*

> When you encounter your enemy's ox or ass wandering, you must take it back. When you see the ass of your enemy lying under its burden and would refrain from raising it, you must nevertheless help raise it.
>
> —Exodus 23:4–5

Recently, I wrote here about the successful first meeting of our series "Meet the Imam," in which local Jews came to learn basic Islam from the imam of the mosque in a nearby Arab town. For the second session, scheduled for last week, I invited an imam who had been recommended to me. A Ph.D. in chemistry, he also teaches in the gifted program of the school in his village. The topic was to be "Family in Islam." The date turned out to be about a week into the Israeli incursion into Gaza. I called him a few days before to confirm the details, sent out publicity, and bought the cake. By 8:30 on the appointed evening, people had assembled—but there was no sign of the speaker. I called him:

"Hi, Ahmed?"

"Yes."

"This is Marc at Shorashim. Are you on your way here?"

"I'm not coming."

"I don't understand."

"When tanks are firing at children, I can't come and discuss Islam and family life."

"I see. I'm sorry you didn't call me—the people are all waiting here."

"I just assumed you would have canceled. How could we meet now?"

"I would have called you. Seems to me it's a time like this when it's important to meet."

"Besides, will you guarantee my safety if I come?"

"Yes, of course! Shall we wait?"

"No, I'm not coming. This is not the time."

As of this writing (by the time you read it the situation may be different), this war is hugely popular among the Jewish public. Expressions of opposition are rare. The press, politicians across the spectrum, and public opinion are united in solid support of our "boys" as they pound Hamas, finally giving vent to our feelings of frustration and persecution—and identification with the residents of the border region—after the irritating and frightening experience of eight years of rocket bombardments that we couldn't seem to stop. Everyone is competing to send gifts to the soldiers, host children from the border towns, and perform other acts of support. Periodically, we read that the ministers in the government are at odds with each other regarding the goals of the operation and the preferred outcome, but as long as we are "winning," and our casualties are few, the tabloids are cheering us with color photos of smiling soldiers enthusiastically going off to save the homeland, and heartrending accounts of the heroic casualties.

There are, of course, Jews who are ambivalent, or who think that the massive destruction, injuries, and deaths in Gaza (which are not shown on our TV) will only strengthen the forces opposed to peace in the long run. There are those who say that the "withdrawal" from Gaza in 2005 was somewhat of an illusion, as we kept Gaza under siege. There are those who see the attempt to unseat Hamas (an organization Israel supported and funded in the 1980s, to undermine Fatah) as another attempt to control Arab governments that is destined to fail like all the others. But they are all keeping a low profile.

I guess history will show who was right. Meanwhile, the Arab citizens of Israel are torn. They are angry, depressed, and sad. They cannot help but identify with the suffering of Gazans—yet to express such identification is to brand themselves as traitors to the war effort (which, of course, would only confirm the long-held suspicions of many Jews). No matter how justified this war, no matter how evil Hamas, it is hard not to sympathize with the pain of the Israeli Arabs as their multiple identities collide head-on. I fear that this operation may have, in the long term, unintended and unhappy effects on the fragile fabric of Israeli society. Hopefully, I'll be proven wrong.

PART VI

Flora of Israel

47. Hyssop Season *(April 3, 2005)*

This week was Shabbat Parah, a week before the Shabbat on which Rosh Chodesh Nisan is proclaimed. The special Torah reading, from Numbers 19, describes the strange ritual of the red heifer, performed to purify anyone who had come into contact with a dead body. The ritual makes prominent use of hyssop, a well-known herb that grows wild in the mountainous areas of Israel. According to the instructions in the Torah, it is both burned with the sacrifice and used to sprinkle the purifying solution where needed. Apparently, hyssop was seen as some kind of spiritual disinfectant:

> Purge me with hyssop till I am pure; wash me till I am whiter than snow.
>
> —Psalm 51:9

Hyssop, *eizov* in Hebrew, is the common name of Syrian marjoram, which has small gray-green leaves on a woody stem, grows about a foot high, and grows wild in the same environment as sage, oregano, and peppermint, all of which bear a certain resemblance to each other. It has a distinctive, pungent aroma, released when you brush past the plant and bruise the leaves. Just now, as the rainy season is ending, these plants are at their peak; by the end of spring they seem to disappear, keeping a low profile until next winter.

A passage describing Solomon's wisdom seems to imply that hyssop is among the humblest of plants: "He discoursed about trees, from the cedar in Lebanon to the hyssop that grows out of the wall" (I Kings 5:13). This, in turn, gave rise to the expression, appearing in the Talmud, in a eulogy for a great Rabbi, "If a fire breaks out among the cedars, what will the hyssop of the wall do?" (*Moed Katan* 25b). This, in turn, has become a popular proverb, roughly translated as: "If great men stumble, what can you expect of us small fry?"

Like so many wild herbs—especially those with a strong fragrance—hyssop is reputed to have many medicinal qualities, and the inhabitants of the region use it to cure everything from nasal congestion to heart disease. In fact, it does contain biologically active compounds, and an extract of the leaves is used in various antifungal and antiseptic ointments, mouthwashes, and the like.

This plant is best known, however, by its Arabic name, *za'atar*. It is used as a seasoning in just about every Middle Eastern recipe, generally as the chief ingredient of a mixture—also called *za'atar*—containing salt, sumac, sesame seeds, and a few other herbs. This mix is sprinkled on pita moistened with olive oil, on *labaneh* (yogurt cheese), on chumus, salads, meat, and so on. It is one of the characteristic tastes of Middle Eastern cooking.

The conditions in the central Galilee are ideal for hyssop to grow, and it is easy to find anywhere you hike in this season. Indeed, our mountainside here at Shorashim is known as a prime source of the herb (this year, a couple of very healthy specimens have come up in our backyard). In Arab village culture, one of the main agricultural tasks of the early spring is to comb the open areas outside the villages, collecting various seasonal wild herbs and vegetables. On our Shabbat walk we often run into whole families out harvesting—the parents drag the gunny sacks, and the kids fan out over the green mountainsides with knives and hoes to harvest the spring greens. Since hyssop and other herbs have a short season, they need to harvest a lot to dry a whole year's supply.

Unfortunately, this traditional folk idyll has run up against modernity in a couple of ways: The land around the villages is no longer just open space—much of it is now occupied by Jewish communities, who do not always look with favor upon visitors digging up the vegetation. When we encounter harvesters, there are some of us who will demand that they leave the property and threaten to call the police; there are others who say "Good morning" and keep walking. Moreover, because of the increase in population, the shrinking of habitats (and, apparently, the market for Galilean hyssop in the Persian Gulf), there is a real danger to the plant population, so Israel has declared it an endangered species; that is, forbidden to pick. An obvious solution would seem to be cultivating hyssop—it isn't hard to grow. But the cultural conflict here is deeper, relating to the Arabs' traditional lifestyle, and their utilization (not necessarily legal ownership) of the resources of the commons, the open land.

I wonder if the apocalyptic Orthodox Zionists and evangelical Christians busy trying to breed red heifers have given thought to ensuring a stable supply of hyssop.

48. Seven Species I—Barley *(April 11, 2004)*

In the description in the Torah of the agricultural richness of the Land of Israel, the seven principal crops are mentioned:

> A land of wheat and barley, of vines, figs, and pomegranates, a land of olive trees and [date] honey.
> —Deuteronomy 8:8

Since the beginning of Zionist settlement of the land, many

new cash crops have been introduced to the Israeli agricultural economy; some have become symbols of modern Israel in the eyes of the world, like sabras and oranges; others simply make their quiet contribution to the economy and the quality of life (cucumbers, avocadoes, melons, and many others). Israel is by no means self-sufficient in grain, and we eat dried figs imported from Turkey. Nevertheless, the seven species remain not only a traditional concept, but still symbolize for us the native produce of this land, and connect the modern landscape to the biblical description. The actual ritual for the bringing of the first fruits on Shavuot is described in Deuteronomy 26. Later, the Mishnah specifies: "The first fruits offering must be taken only from the seven species" (*Bikkurim* 1:3).

This season, leading up to Shavuot, seems an appropriate time to examine the seven species and their place in our tradition.

> The Lord spoke to Moses, saying: Speak to the Israelite people and say to them: When you enter the land that I am giving to you and you reap its harvest, you shall bring the first sheaf [*omer*] of your harvest to the priest. He shall elevate the sheaf before the Lord for acceptance in your behalf. . . . Until that very day, you shall eat no bread or parched grain or fresh ears. (Leviticus 23: 9–14)

Barley and wheat have both been cultivated in Israel since ancient times. Barley seems to be associated with a less developed society, growing in poorer soil, requiring less sophisticated agricultural knowledge. It was considered the most basic foodstuff—in assessing the value of a field, one calculated the amount of barley seed needed to seed it (Leviticus 27:16); it was definitely less valuable than wheat (II Kings 7:1). Later, in *Sifrei B'midbar* (89), we read: "Why are you eating barley bread?" "Because I have no wheat bread!"

Barley ripens earlier than wheat (Exodus 9:31). It is the barley harvest that is referred to in the above passage about the *omer* offering. The practice was to cut the first sheaves of barley the day before Pesach, and to bring an offering from this early harvest on the second day of the festival. Until this was brought, it was forbidden to eat from this new crop. This perhaps helps to explain the elimination of all old grain products in preparation for Pesach: We clear away the old to make way for the new; then for the week of Pesach we eat only matzah (made from a portion of last year's crop that was carefully protected all year from dampness and from contamination by leavening), and afterwards we may enjoy the new crop freely, in any form.

The barley harvest goes on for nearly two months before the wheat ripens. Barley is no longer a significant crop here; it is used primarily as animal feed. As I drive through the Jezreel Valley each week on my way to a teaching assignment, I notice broad fields of wheat that are now characteristically pale green, waving in the breeze—they have not started to turn golden yet.

None of the above was relevant, of course, during the forty years the Israelites wandered in the desert, for there they ate manna all the time. The first thing they did after crossing the Jordan River behind Joshua was to observe Pesach, and . . .

> On the day after the Passover offering, on that very day, they ate of the produce of the country, unleavened bread and parched grain. On that same day, when they ate of the produce of the land, the manna ceased. (Joshua 5:11–12)

So it seems that one of our first experiences upon arrival in the Land of Israel was to make the transition from manna to barley, to put down roots, to become dependent on the land (and our working of it); once we got here, there was no more free lunch.

49. Seven Species II—Wheat *(April 18, 2004)*

And from the day on which you bring the sheaf [*omer*] of elevation offering—the day after the sabbath—you shall count off
seven weeks. They must be complete: you must count until the
day after the seventh week—fifty days; then you shall bring an
offering of new grain to the Eternal.

—Leviticus 23:15–16

Once the first sheaves of the barley harvest were brought to the priest
as an offering on the second day of Pesach, seven weeks were counted
off (what has become known as the "counting of the *omer*"), during
which time, apparently, the barley harvest was completed as the wheat
ripened. The fiftieth day was the festival of Shavuot, at which an offering of leavened bread was to be made, baked from the new grain. This
was the beginning of the wheat harvest, and this bread represented an
initial offering, "first fruits" of that harvest: "You shall observe the feast
of Shavuot, of the first fruits of the wheat harvest . . ." (Exodus 34:22).

Wheat, it seems, represented prosperity and stability, and served
as a symbol for abundance of food in biblical poetry (Deuteronomy
32:14; Psalm 81:17; Psalm 147:14). In the Bible, "fine bread" and
"fine flour" are always made from wheat.

In the Mishnah (*P'sachim* 2:5), five types of grain are specified as
being suitable for making into matzah—and, it follows, susceptible
to becoming *chameitz* (leavened bread). As is often the case, the exact botanical definitions of the five grains are open to some debate,
but it seems that they are barley, oats (which has never been a major
crop here), and three different species of wheat. Similarly, only bread
made from these five grains is covered by *HaMotzi,* and requires the
full *Birkat HaMazon* (Grace After Meals).

Today, 85 percent of Israel's wheat is imported. And yet, this land
may have been the birthplace of wheat: Aaron Aaronsohn (1876–
1919), son of farmers from the First Aliyah in Zichron Ya'akov, studied

agronomy in France and returned to engage in research on the genetics of the native varieties of wheat. In 1906 he discovered strains thought to be among the most primitive in the world, containing the basic gene pool from which later domesticated varieties developed.

Recently, we joined our daughter on a field trip with her economic botany class, and visited the wheat research center at Tel Aviv University, where we saw cold rooms holding thousands of samples of wheat seeds, some of them taken from local wild varieties that have already become extinct in nature. This genetic treasure has already been exploited to develop, through scientific crossbreeding, varieties resistant to newly emerging viruses and other pests. Thus, while Israel must import wheat to eat, it exports wheat genes and expertise—even to Iowa. With the controversial rise of mass-scale industrial farming and of genetically modified crops, this project—along with other seed-saving efforts large and small—can be seen as a kind of Noah's Ark, seeking to save us from unforeseen disasters generated by our own cleverness.

> [What was] the tree from which Adam ate? . . . Rabbi Judah says: It was wheat, for a baby isn't able to say "Daddy" and "Mommy" until he is old enough to eat cereal. . . . [that is, wheat is the source of knowledge of right and wrong]. (Babylonian Talmud, *Sanhedrin* 70b)

Perhaps, in view of the central nutritional and economic status of wheat, and its role as a symbol of stable, cultivated abundance here in *Eretz Yisrael,* this midrash is not so far-fetched.

50. Seven Species III—Grapes *(April 25, 2004)*

In Numbers 13 we read that when Moses sent in the twelve spies to scout out the land of Canaan, ". . . it happened to be the season of the first ripe grapes" (verse 20).

They reached the wadi Eshcol, and there they cut down a branch with a single cluster of grapes—it had to be borne on a carrying frame by two of them—and some pomegranates and figs. That place was named the wadi Eshcol because of the cluster that the Israelites cut down there.

—Numbers 13:23–24

The pictogram of two people carrying a huge bunch of grapes on a pole between them is, of course, the familiar insignia of the Israel Ministry of Tourism—after all, the spies were the first tourists to visit Israel. Grapes, the third of the seven species (Deuteronomy 8:8), have always served as a symbol par excellence of the agricultural plenty of *Eretz Yisrael*.

On top of our hillside here at Shorashim there is an ancient *gat* (winepress) cut into the limestone. About ten years ago the bar mitzvah class excavated it with an archaeologist, as a class project, cutting away the overgrowth and clearing away fill. It is about time to do it again—the weeds have taken over. Winepresses like these are a common feature of the landscape, and every amateur archaeologist can identify them. It is interesting to conjecture who carved it there. Muslims are forbidden to drink wine. Every Arab house has a grape arbor on the roof, and in late summer the heavy clusters are a beautiful sight as you walk through the villages; but these grapes are only for eating, not for winemaking. Perhaps there was a Christian community here in Byzantine times; perhaps a Jewish village.

The grapevine may have been a central feature of the landscape here forever, but by the end of the nineteenth century, after over a thousand years of Muslim domination, grape cultivation was mostly limited to small local vineyards and home arbors. It was the Rothschilds who revived the ancient heritage of viticulture here. When Baron Edmond de Rothschild decided to help the Zionist settlers establish an economic base in the late nineteenth century, as the owner of Château

Lafite Winery, he found it natural to try to nurture the wine industry here, sending cuttings and experts. It took awhile, and a certain amount of trial and error, but the project ultimately succeeded, and every Zionist is familiar with Carmel wines from the Rothschilds' wineries at Zichron Ya'akov and Rishon Letzion; for years, Diaspora Jews bought them as a gesture of solidarity, regardless of their quality. Only twenty years ago, it was almost impossible to find any wines in the shops here except a handful of rather boring Carmel varieties. In recent years, however, the industry has grown and the market has opened up; now there are many wineries large and small, and new varieties of grapes grown in the Golan, the Galilee, Judah, and the coastal plain. The supermarket wine aisle feels almost like America (well, not really), with a broad range of tastes and prices.

Many people—often including myself—are nostalgic for the "good old days" in Israel, when there were just three soft drinks and two kinds of bread, before commercialization and globalization, when everyone ate falafel instead of McDonald's. But I don't think there is anyone who doesn't take pleasure from the development of the wine industry. The "good life" as symbolized by the supermarket wine aisle is the same "good life" the spies saw three thousand years ago. And it's worth noting that the ultimate good life is described by the prophet Micah (4:3–4) thus:

> . . . Nation shall not take up sword against nation;
> They shall never again know war;
> But every man shall sit under his grapevine or fig tree
> With no one to disturb him . . .

51. Seven Species IV—Figs *(May 2, 2004)*

The first tree mentioned by name in the Bible is, of course, the fig, whose leaves Adam and Eve sewed together to cover their nakedness

(Genesis 3:7). Grapes and wheat have come to symbolize the agriculture of *Eretz Yisrael:* Both are species that have been actively cultivated for thousands of years; both are associated with culture, with technology, with civilization. The fig, on the other hand, the fourth of the "seven species" (Deuteronomy 8:8), seems more a symbol of the land itself. Figs in Israel don't grow in neat rows, and have not been adapted to modern agriculture. If you want to see fig plantations, where the fruit is mass-produced for drying, you have to travel to the Turkish countryside. In fact, while fresh figs are plentiful here in summer, dried figs are not produced here at all; when we buy dried figs for our Tu BiSh'vat seder, the only ones available are imported from Turkey. Here, they grow as lone trees, in the courtyards of houses, along streams, on the sites of abandoned villages. They hardly seem to be a product of human cultivation—they seem to be a natural part of the landscape.

Indeed, in folklore, fig trees grow not as a product of human efforts, but in defiance of them: In the old city of Acre there is a large fig tree growing out of a stone wall, which according to legend overcame all attempts by the caliph to have it cut down, miraculously sprouting anew after each attack.

Among the wild raspberry and other weeds that persistently sprout in the rocky terrace in our front yard, a few years ago a little plant appeared with leaves that looked like fig leaves. We left it alone. It is now a stunted, weirdly shaped sapling, whose branches, instead of growing upward, curve downward from the terrace in which it is rooted. And if we had any doubts about its identity, this spring it has produced a fruit that is clearly an unripe fig. It turns out that this is not the first fig tree to grow out of a rock:

> "He fed him honey from the crag" [Deuteronomy 32:13]
> refers to Sichni and its environs: It is told that Rabbi Judah said to his son, "Go and bring me dried figs from the barrel." He [came back and] said, "Father, there is only

honey there." R. Judah said, "Stick your hand into the honey and bring up the figs." (*Sifrei D'varim, Haazinu* 316)

Sichni is generally thought to be Sachnin, the Arab town located about five minutes' drive from Shorashim. In the Talmud, Sichni and its valley are often used to symbolize the bounty of the land, the richness and high quality of the agricultural produce of Israel. The honey from the crag (and in Psalm 81:17, "honey from the rock") seems to be understood as fig honey, the sweet, syrupy juice of this fruit. Hence, the lone fig on the stunted tree sprouting from the rock in our yard is no less than the referent of the biblical image in Deuteronomy and Psalms, "honey from the rock."

In summer, preteenage Arab boys endanger their lives and ours, standing on the shoulder of the highway, holding out buckets of fresh-picked ripe figs, oozy in the sun and sickeningly sweet, the taste of decadence. While modernization is evident everywhere in Arab villages in Israel, there are still many homes with a yard graced with fruit trees and a grape arbor. Even families who have long since left agriculture as a livelihood preserve the tradition of growing fruit and vegetables for their own use and sometimes a little extra income. Harvesting and selling the figs is a good summer occupation for the kids. Why are figs not a significant commercial crop here? One reason, apparently, is that a tree's fruit ripens over a long period, not all at once, so the figs must be harvested by hand, one at a time, re-picking the same tree day after day; only kids have the time.

Why is the Torah likened to a fig tree? All other trees— the olive, the grape, the date—are harvested all at once; but the fig tree is harvested little by little. So it is with the Torah: Today you learn a little; tomorrow you learn a lot; the Torah is not learned in one year nor even in two years. Hence the verse, "He who tends a fig tree will enjoy its fruit" [Proverbs 27:18] refers to the Torah as fruit. (*B'midbar Rabbah* 12:9)

Text and land—each helps us find meaning in the other.

52. Seven Species V—Pomegranates *(May 9, 2004)*

Of the seven species that symbolize the bounty of *Eretz Yisrael* (Deuteronomy 8:8), six are staple foodstuffs: two grains, wine and oil, and the two indigenous sweet fruits that can be easily dried and stored—figs and dates. That leaves one species that doesn't seem to fit this utilitarian pattern: the pomegranate. In the picture of fertility, of plenty, of filled silos and storerooms that the Bible presents, "a land where you may eat food without stint, where you will lack nothing . . ." (Deuteronomy 8:9), the pomegranate represents something altogether different: not a staple, but a delicacy; not our daily bread, but a strikingly beautiful and tempting fruit, whose bright flowers beautify the late spring and whose crimson tart-sweet juice is the taste of the end of summer.

Aside from its occasional mention in passages listing the native fruits of the land, the main appearance of the pomegranate in the Bible is in Song of Songs:

> Your lips are like a crimson thread, your mouth is lovely.
> Your brow behind your veil like a pomegranate split open.
> (4:3 and 6:7)

> Your limbs are an orchard of pomegranates and of all luscious fruits, of henna and of nard. (4:13)

> Let us go early to the vineyards; let us see if the vine has
> flowered, if its blossoms have opened, if the pomegranates

are in bloom. There I will give my love to you. (7:13 and 6:11)

I would lead you, I would bring you to the house of my mother, of her who bore me—I would let you drink of the spiced wine, of my pomegranate juice. (8:2)

Interestingly, in Greek mythology, too, the pomegranate serves as a symbol of temptation: When Zeus negotiates the release of Persephone from Hades, who has kidnapped and spirited her to his realm, the condition for her release is that she eat nothing from there. But Hades gives her a pomegranate, and she can't resist eating some of its pips; so she is bound to spend a third of each year there—which is why we have winter.

There is something about the pomegranate's rich color, its abundant sweet juice, its distinctive, graceful shape, that has turned it into a symbol not so much of plenty, but of beauty and sensuality. The shape was a common decorative motif: The priests' robes were bordered with pomegranate-shaped decorations (Exodus 28:33, for example); similarly, the pillars of Solomon's temple were adorned with bronze pomegranates (I Kings 7:18–20).

Rabbinic references to pomegranates tend to sidestep the sensual connotation of the image, and to focus on the geometry: the tight-packed multitude of pips (I have been told that there are always 613 pips in a pomegranate, but I've seen no source for this—and I've never counted) as an image of being "filled up"—with mitzvot, with Torah, and the like. Thus, it is a widespread custom here to serve pomegranate on Rosh Ha-Shanah, parallel to apples and honey, and to ask God to grant us a new year as full of blessings as the pomegranate is full of pips.

Perhaps the pomegranate comes to remind us that this is not only a land of plenty, but a land of beauty; that God has seen not only to our physical needs, but to our aesthetic ones, too. The native fruits of the land provide not only images of prosperity, but also images of love and of sensuality. Our rootedness in this place touches every aspect of our humanness. "Man does not live on bread alone" (Deuteronomy 8:3), but on pomegranates as well.

53. Seven Species VI—Olives *(May 16, 2004)*

Not only is the olive tree one of the most distinctive features of the landscape of the whole Mediterranean region, with its silvery-green leaves and beautifully gnarled trunks; not only is the olive a staple of the diet of the region—as an easily preserved (by salt curing) vegetable and as the prime cooking oil; not only does the olive serve as an important cosmetic and medicinal oil; but it was, for thousands of years, the major light source, the fuel for the ubiquitous oil lamps found in archaeological excavations from every historical period. It is not surprising, therefore, that olive oil also took on religious significance, as the anointing oil for priests and kings: In ancient Israel kings were not crowned, they were anointed. And, of course, the sacred lamp in the Temple, the menorah, was fueled with the finest and purest olive oil, specially certified by the priests: "You shall further instruct the Israelites to bring you clear oil of beaten olives for lighting, for kindling lamps regularly. Aaron and his sons shall set them up in the Tent of Meeting . . ." (Exodus 27:20–21).

Both texts and stones attest to the significance of olive oil in the everyday life and economy of *Eretz Yisrael.* The Mishnah (*Menachot* 8:4) explains in detail the process for producing olive oil and the characteristics of the nine different grades, based on three quality levels (tree-ripened, ripened on the roof after picking, and stored until they go soft), and three processing methods for each (crushing and allowing the oil to flow out without pressure; pressing the crushed olives to squeeze out more oil; and grinding and re-pressing to squeeze out the residue). For each quality level, only the oil extracted by the first method, without pressure, is fine enough for lighting. The distinctive remains of oil presses are found in archaeological sites all over the country. There are a number of modern oil mills here in the Galilee. The method has remained constant over the centuries—only the materials and the energy source have changed: The olives are crushed and then placed in flexible baskets; pressure is applied to squeeze out the oil and water, which are then separated by gravity or centrifugation.

And olive oil, of course, plays a central role in the story of Chanukah: While the Book of Maccabees—the historical account of the Maccabean revolt against the Seleucids in the second century B.C.E.—does not mention the well-known miracle of the little jug of oil that burned for eight days, the Talmud (edited about five hundred years later) tells the story:

> When the Greeks entered the Temple, they desecrated all the oil that was there. When the Hasmoneans overcame them, they looked and found only one jug of oil, enough to light [the menorah] for one day; but a miracle occurred and they lit [the menorah] from this [oil] for eight days . . . (Babylonian Talmud, *Shabbat* 21b)

Why eight days? What happened at the end of eight days? Did they obtain more oil? If so, why did it take eight days? It turns out that these questions were asked in the past, and answered.

In Deuteronomy 33:24, Moses blesses the tribe of Asher thus: "Most blessed of sons be Asher; may he be the favorite of his brothers; may he dip his foot in oil." The territory of Asher is the western Galilee, and is indeed known as a source of fine and plentiful olive oil. Later, Mishnah *Menachot* 8:3 states that the finest oil, used for the Temple, was from Tekoah. Most sources identify Tekoah as a town in Judea, southeast of Jerusalem. However, in the responsa of the *gaonim* (the chief Rabbis of Babylonia in the Middle Ages), Tekoah is taken as referring to a town in the Galilee—apparently based on the blessing of Asher in Deuteronomy. This same source goes on to suggest that Tekoah was a four-day journey from Jerusalem. Thus, once the Temple was reconquered and purified, it took eight days for a messenger to get to Tekoah in the Galilee, obtain a stock of pure oil, and return to refuel the menorah.

The Rabbis may have tried to "dehistoricize" Chanukah by substituting the miracle of the oil for the victory celebration described in the Book of Maccabees, but they couldn't "degeographize" it: The miracle itself became another expression of our rootedness in the landscape of *Eretz Yisrael*.

54. Seven Species VII—Dates *(May 23, 2004)*

On our community's annual Yom HaAtzma-ut excursion a few weeks ago, we were hiking along the Jordan River above the Sea of Galilee, when we came upon a row of beehives next to a fence—and on the other side of the fence a herd of cows grazing among the spring wildflowers. Sure enough, someone pointed out, the "land flowing with milk and honey" (Deuteronomy 6:3 and many other places in the Bible). The seventh of the products that symbolize the abundance of *Eretz Yisrael* (Deuteronomy 8:8) is honey. However, just what is meant by honey is not clear, as can be seen from the argument between two second-century Rabbis (Midrash *Mechilta D'Rabbi Shimon bar Yochai* 13):

> Rabbi Eliezer says that *milk and honey* refers to fruit milk and date honey; Rabbi Akiba says that *milk* means actual milk . . . , and that *honey* means forest [i.e., bee] honey.

While there are a few specific references to bee honey in the Bible (for example, Judges 14:8 and I Samuel 14:25–29), most commentators agree with Rabbi Eliezer that the honey included in the seven species and in the phrase *flowing with milk and honey* is, in fact, date honey, a syrup produced by cooking and straining crushed dates. This syrup, also called *silan,* has been widely used as a sweetener since ancient times. The identification of the date palm (*tamar*) as one of the seven species makes sense, in view of the importance of the date palm in the economy, diet, and landscape of the Middle East since time immemorial. The economic and symbolic significances of this species intersect nicely in the following midrash on Psalm 92:13, "The righteous bloom like a date palm":

> Just as no part of the date palm is useless—the dates are eaten, the branches are waved during *hallel* (i.e., the *lulav* of Sukkot), the fronds are used to roof the sukkah, the fibers are twisted into rope, the leaves woven into sieves, the trunks serve as roof beams of houses—so no one of the Jewish people is useless—some are knowledgeable in Bible, some in Mishnah, some in Talmud, some in aggadah [i.e., maybe no one knows everything, but everybody knows something useful—everyone has a role in the community]. (*B'reishit Rabbah* 41)

The date palm has always been a common motif in art—appearing on ancient coins and in relief carvings in synagogues. Moreover, of all of the seven species, it is the only one that became a common name. There are several Tamars in the Bible, and the name has remained popular throughout the generations—I think it is one of the few women's names that one encounters in Israel today in every generation and in every ethnic population. It is a name that combines a sense of history, of biblical roots, with a physical referent that is very much a part of the modern landscape of Israel. And I guess the associations are hard to fault: strength, grace, sweetness, fertility, usefulness—who wouldn't want their daughter to be a Tamar?

Ashkenazi Jews base their recipes for Pesach *charoset* on ground apples; for Jews from the Middle East, dates are usually the basis—and Iraqi *charoset* is a paste made simply by mixing date syrup with ground nuts.

If olives connect us with the Mediterranean basin, dates tie us to the Middle East. The date palm grows mainly in the hot valleys, around the Sea of Galilee (Kinneret), in the Jordan Valley, along the Dead Sea. Interestingly, natural as they seem here, these trees require intensive care, and by the early twentieth century, due to neglect, the plantations in Palestine were much reduced. Ben Zion Yisraeli, a founder of Kibbutz Kinneret, smuggled hundreds of seedlings into the country from Iraq, and the industry was rejuvenated.

Yisraeli's comrade at Kinneret, the "poet laureate" of the pioneers, Rachel Bluwstein, wrote poems about her adopted landscape, which became and remained core documents of Israeli culture. One of her most famous poems, "Kinneret," a song that is still popular, contains the verse:

> There on the shore of the sea stands a low-hanging palm,
> Its hair disheveled like that of a mischievous child,
> Who has slid down to splash his feet in the waters of
>   the Kinneret.

You can visit the Kinneret cemetery today where Yisraeli and Rachel are buried along with many of the famous names of the socialist Second Aliyah. And just there, on the shore of the sea, stands a low-hanging date palm.

55. Sabra Dreams *(April 13, 2003)*

We all have our crosses to bear and I guess you are mine. I just can't take it with the straight-faced unconcern of a sabra.
—Leon Uris, *Exodus* (Doubleday & Company, 1958)

I was pleased to note the other day that the pads of the sabra plant in our yard are covered with buds that look like tiny clusters of purplish spikes.

When the pioneers of Shorashim came to this hillside in 1985, most of them envisioned the future of the community as a model high-tech commune, bringing together Zionist idealism, American pluralism, and sophisticated technological know-how to generate happiness and prosperity. There was a small minority, however, who were not swept away by dreams of the electronic jackpot, but were attracted by the classic Zionist ideal of working the land. Despite the small and rocky plot assigned to Shorashim, they nurtured the dream of agricultural productivity as a means of livelihood, personal fulfillment, and bonding to the Land of Israel. And so, after some consultation with agronomists, they received permission to plant the flat surface of the Shorashim ridge with a few fields of sabra cacti.

The prickly pear cactus was imported to Europe in the eighteenth century. It was prized for the red dye, cochineal, that the native Americans made from it (actually, from an insect that infested it). The plants spread around the Mediterranean basin; the forbidding stands of thorny sabras quickly became a major feature of the landscape, serving as a living barbed-wire fence in Arab villages. Based on the medieval Arabic term for the aloe plant, *tsaber,* the local Arabs called the import *tsaber;* this became *tsabar* in Hebrew. In colloquial Hebrew and Arabic, the plant is referred to as *tsabras* or *sabra.* Today, the hedges often remain and thrive even in places where the villages have been destroyed and/or abandoned. During the summer, bright flowers sprout from the edges of the leaf-pads, becoming dark-red oblong fruits about the size of a medium pear, protruding from the padlike fingers of a hand. While you can buy them in fruit markets, most people buy them from Arab boys on the street, who harvest them using a tin can nailed to a long stick and then wear plastic gloves to hold them while cutting off the prickly skin. They have the consistency of a peach, and are sweet and full of hard little seeds.

To the immigrants from Eastern Europe, the sabra cactus was exotic and Middle Eastern—they never imagined its New World origins. It seemed a fitting image for their identity as New Jews. The New Jew was the opposite of the Old Jew. He (and she) was suntanned and fearless, at home in nature, strong and self-confident to the point of rudeness—yet humane and generous.

There are a few ironies in the fact that the sabra, an import grown mainly by Arabs, came to serve as the symbol and colloquial name for the native-born Jewish Israeli, based on the image of the New Jew: prickly and forbidding on the outside but soft and sweet on the inside. Or, at least, that's how we wanted to see ourselves.

The sabras planted in the fields of Shorashim were a new variety, bred to be spineless or almost so (is there another irony here?). Fields were plowed and planted, and irrigation lines laid. However, within a few years it became clear that the match of variety, soil, and other conditions was not a good one, and the cost of caring for the plants would never be recovered in the income from the fruit. The water was turned off and the fields abandoned. The cacti are still there, but seem to have grown very slowly if at all, and are in many places completely overgrown with wild raspberries and other shrubs and weeds.

Shortly after we moved to Shorashim, about ten years ago, I snapped off a pad from one of the abandoned sabras and laid it on the ground in our garden. It rooted, and a new plant began to grow out of it. Today it is a dense mass of pads about ten feet high, and has given rise to a number of offspring in the farther reaches of our yard. A certain family member has insisted that I break off pads that are encroaching on the territory of neighboring rose and hibiscus bushes. I find the growth of the sabra fascinating to watch, and it is probably my favorite of the plants in our garden. Each spring, little magenta buds pop up along the upper edges of the pads. There seems to be no pattern or system—some pads will sprout one bud, some six, some none. Most of these turn out to be new pads, but a few will become flowers—last year we harvested dozens of delicious fruits. And so it goes from year to year—exponentially, I suppose—so that our yard is dominated by this weird plant—trunk/branches/leaves all in one. On a trip to Mexico a few years ago, we learned that the pads are commonly eaten as a vegetable, and we learned how to cook them (they have a slimy consistency, like okra); periodically we harvest a few to use in salads or cooked vegetable dishes. We usually cut them in strips—they fulfill the role of a slightly sour green bean. I tried to offer some to Arab construction workers working at our house, but they refused, declaring that the pads couldn't possibly be edible.

56. Beautiful Trees *(October 9, 2005)*

On the first day you shall take the fruit of *hadar* trees, branches of palm trees, boughs of leafy trees, and willows of the brook, and you shall rejoice before the Lord your God seven days.
—Leviticus 23:40

Hadar is generally translated as "goodly," or beautiful. Traditionally, the biblical reference to "the fruit of *hadar* trees" is taken as the *etrog,* or citron. The fragrant *etrog* and the three other species constituting the *lulav* are the central symbols of Sukkot—and judging from the carvings and mosaics found in ancient synagogues, they have also served as symbols of Judaism in general. The *etrog,* originally from China, made its way to the Middle East via Persia during the Hellenistic period. While rabbinic texts raise the possibility that one might consider using a quince or a pomegranate for Sukkot rejoicing, the Rabbis reject it, as already by their time the *etrog* was taken for granted. Over time, "the fruit of *hadar* trees" came to refer to all varieties of citrus fruit; today *pri hadar* (*hadar* fruit) simply means citrus in colloquial Hebrew.

The Rothschilds' agronomists' influence was felt in this field as well as in viticulture, as they encouraged the planting of lemon, orange, and grapefruit groves in order to produce an export commodity. Indeed, until about twenty years ago, citrus fruit symbolized the agricultural bounty of the modern State of Israel. The Jaffa orange was a kind of unofficial national symbol, and the citrus orchards along the coastal plain were one of the most memorable sights (and smells) that greeted the tourist upon landing. I have a visceral memory of driving away from the airport on a warm, humid night with the mix of orange perfume and exhaust fumes blowing in the window. Finding Jaffa oranges in our local supermarkets always gave us American Jews warm, proud feelings.

However, the world has moved on and so has Israel. The acreage devoted to citrus orchards has been in decline for two decades, as the trees are removed to make room for shopping malls, housing developments, and more exotic, profitable fruits and vegetables. Water for irrigation, despite all our brilliant technology (drip irrigation is an Israeli invention), is becoming scarcer and more expensive; Spain, Italy, Morocco, and South Africa are powerful competitors on the world market; agricultural labor is expensive. With the globalization of economy and culture, Israel's unique relationship to citrus fruit has faded. I remember when there were three bottled soft drinks in Israel: sweetened grapefruit juice, sweetened orange juice, and lemon-lime soda—all locally made. Today the soft drink cooler at any fast-food stand is packed with dozens of choices, most of them imported brands. The model of the pioneer who would make the desert green and productive has given way to the model of the high-tech engineer or entrepreneur who will build Israel's leadership in the world market for medical electronics, communications software, and the like. Today agricultural products—including citrus fruit—make up only 3 percent of Israel's total exports.

Sukkot is coming, and even for the high techies among us, our thoughts turn to "the fruit of beautiful trees," the fragrance of the *etrog,* and the pleasant feeling of holding it in our hands— thoughts that bring us back to a preglobal, premodern, elemental connection to the land and its fruits.

PART VII

Israeli Culture

57. Present Arms! *(February 11, 2001)*

[God] said, "Take your son, your only one, Isaac, the one you love, Isaac, and go forth to the land of Moriah. Offer him there as a burnt-offering, on one of the mountains that I will show you."

—Genesis 22:2

Just returned from my son Lev's beret ceremony for paratroopers: graduation from basic training. This is a major rite of passage for Israeli males (except, of course, for the ultra-Orthodox and most Arabs). No matter what you have scheduled for that day, if you tell people you have your son's beret ceremony, you are expected to cancel your plans and go. And so we packed up snacks and umbrellas and picnic blankets and set off for the three-hour drive to Jerusalem, on a cold, showery day. Having done extensive research among veteran parents about the appropriate fare for the postceremony picnic, we stopped at one of the hole-in-the-wall *steakiot* in the Machaneh Yehudah market on the way into town. The proprietors, upon learning our destination, treated us as honored guests, filling Styrofoam containers with salads and sauces and soggy French fries to go with the grilled steaks.

Each branch of the army has its own image and reputation. The paratroopers are considered elite infantry; one has to volunteer, and go through a difficult selection process to be accepted. Many chiefs of staff, including Ariel Sharon, came from this corps. Their famous symbol is their maroon berets. In recent years, parachuting has become less relevant and the average paratrooper will only make three training jumps in the course of his three years of service. The paratroopers hold their beret ceremony at Ammunition Hill, in the northern part of what was the Jordanian side of Jerusalem. The place has mythological status as a site of heroic sacrifice by the paratroopers in 1967. Today there is a memorial museum there and children run through the trenches on family picnics and school trips. As with every myth, there have been attempts now and then to debunk the significance of this narrative, suggesting that the sacrifice was in part due to a mistake on the command level.

Arriving at the park, we found the kid waiting for us in dress uniform, hobbling around painfully like all his colleagues, having marched fifty miles overnight from the coast to Jerusalem—the traditional beret march. After half an hour of stories about the march, and being introduced to the buddies and officers we had heard about for the past six months, the parents were directed to seats in an amphitheater while the army organized the kids into loosely lined-up companies in the center. The potbellied master sergeant called us to order, goose-stepped to the microphone, and emceed the ceremony—flag raising, recognition of outstanding trainees, a trite but appropriate inspirational speech by the base commander, lots of "Company, attention" and "Company, at ease," and then "Company commanders, present berets!"

And then, with Israeli easy-listening songs playing on the loudspeaker, songs that conjured up images of the good old days of heroism and simplicity, each commander—himself just a year older than his charges—presented each new paratrooper with the trademark maroon beret and gave him a slap or a hug of affection. At one point, when the slaps and hugs were taking too long, the master sergeant barked, "Company commanders, hurry up!" Then, "Hatikvah" was sung along with the taped choir, and with a whoop, all the berets were tossed in the air, and the smiling troops hobbled off to dine with their families on lukewarm steaks on the wet grass.

Looking over the crowd, I was reminded again what a great leveler the army is here. The families represented every ethnic and socioeconomic grouping, from professors to executives to laborers, religious and secular, city and kibbutz, left and right. We were jockeying for camera angles, annoyed in a good-natured way by each other's umbrellas. Our kids were learning to depend on each other and support each other, to take responsibility for each other and for all of us in ways that seem unimaginable to me.

As a rite of passage and a leveler, the army, with its silly ceremonies, can make you feel proud. You find yourself kvelling to the taped military march music, and eagerly photographing your kid with his beret and rifle. And you know "We have no choice." You know we have a right to exist. You know history. You know we live in a violent world. And yet you wonder what you are doing, and if it has to be this way. You wonder how our democracy might be if it weren't led by generals. You wonder about the effect of learning how to kill as a rite of passage, as the one thing that unites us. And you wonder how it is that you decided to move to a place where your child is learning hand-to-hand combat while his classmates from elementary school in Philadelphia are learning liberal arts.

And then the kid tells you with great enthusiasm that next week they move on to paratroop training—that is, jumping out of airplanes. And you understand that armies are for kids. And you wonder if it has to be this way.

58. The Home Team *(May 30, 2004)*

Zionism was a revolution against a number of different aspects of Jewish existence: against the oppression of the Diaspora, against the sense that the Jewish people had been excluded from history since losing their national sovereignty, against the definition of Judaism as a religion, and against the negative stereotype of the Jew. Seeing Zionism as a multifaceted revolution can help us understand a number of interesting paradoxes and dilemmas in Israeli life and culture today.

In 1898, at the Second Zionist Congress, Herzl's friend and disciple, Dr. Max Nordau, gave his annual keynote address, which is still remembered for its call for "muscular Judaism":

> Let us once more become deep-chested, sturdy, sharp-eyed men. . . . For no other people will gymnastics fulfill a more educational purpose than for us Jews. It shall straighten us in body and in character. . . . Our new muscle Jews have not yet regained the heroism of our forefathers who in large numbers eagerly entered the sports arenas in order to take part in competition and to pit themselves against the highly trained Hellenistic athletes.

Rebelling against the stereotype of the Jew as weak, timid, pale, spiritual, and unable to defend himself, the Zionist Movement placed a high value on athletics. Before the First World War, a network of Maccabi sports clubs had been established in Europe; these later provided the basis for organized athletic activity in the *Yishuv* (the Zionist community in Palestine). Pale-faced, thick-lensed *yeshivah bochers* were not likely to build a modern state; we needed muscular, bold, natural, self-reliant pioneers to create our new reality. Since all the social and economic life of the *Yishuv* was organized along ideological lines, the Maccabi Union became associated with the General Zionists (one of the forerunners of today's Likud), and in the 1920s a parallel organization arose to serve the needs of the athletes of the left: Hapoel sports clubs were affiliated with the Histadrut labor federation. Today, the professional sports teams of Israel still bear the names of those original ideological athletic unions—Maccabi, Hapoel, and also Beitar, associated with Revisionist Zionism—and thus, we are constantly reminded that soccer and basketball are not just branches of the entertainment industry, but important elements of the Zionist revolution.

A few weeks ago, the national championship in soccer was won by Hapoel Sachnin. Sachnin is an Arab town a few miles from Shorashim, long famous for being the focus of tensions between Israeli Arabs and the Israeli government. The team includes Israeli Arabs and Jews and a few foreign players, and the coach is Jewish. While the fan base is the 23,000 people of Sachnin (over half of whom attended the championship game at a stadium near Tel Aviv) and tens of thousands of Arabs from other towns and villages around the Galilee, there are many loyal and enthusiastic fans among the Jewish population of the region, some of whom joined the all-night dancing in the streets of the town after the victory. Sachnin has a typically high unemployment rate and a run-down infrastructure; the team doesn't even have a regulation soccer stadium and has to play home games elsewhere.

Thus, the Jewish state will be represented next year in the European soccer cup competition by an Arab team, wearing the red uniforms of the socialist Zionist Hapoel, playing for their country, whose flag features a blue Magen David. The media is buzzing with stories about what this means—to the Arabs, to Israel, to the conflict. Does the victory symbolize integration and mutual respect based on merit or does it provide a convenient distraction from the ongoing reality of discrimination and marginalization? Do sports really matter? Will the team sing "Hatikvah"?

Herzl and Nordau saw glorious visions of the Zionist future. I wonder if they could have envisioned the president of Israel presenting the championship cup to Hapoel Sachnin.

[*Author's Note:* In 2007, the Sheikhdom of Qatar donated funds for Sachnin to build a regulation soccer stadium.]

59. Dig We Must *(August 15, 2004)*

Better late than never, the Public Works Authority is finally converting the busy grade-level railroad crossing at the eastern entrance to Acre into a viaduct. This is a major project that will involve many months of drilling, pouring concrete, redirecting traffic, and so on. Recently, I noticed in the middle of the excavations the telltale canopies of sunscreen fabric that mark an archaeological excavation. There, surrounded by massive drilling and earthmoving equipment, sat a group of workers applying hand trowels and whisk brooms to the sandy soil. This is a "rescue dig": If any hint of ancient occupation is encountered in the process of excavating for a construction project, the Antiquities Authority moves in to investigate and document the site before it is destroyed. On several occasions foundation digging has revealed rich finds, as in the case of a mosaic floor that turned up in Lod a couple of years ago. The antiquities are so dense in this country that the sight of the archaeologists on their hands and knees, scraping away in the middle of a highway paving project, hardly even attracts notice. We take it for granted.

We have taken our archaeology seriously for a long time. Sometime around 625 B.C.E., young King Josiah ordered a large-scale remodeling project in the Temple. In the course of the work by "carpenters, laborers, and masons," it seems that an ancient scroll was uncovered. The high priest gave it to the king's representative, who read it to the king, who tore his clothes in grief and declared,

"Great indeed must be the wrath of the Lord that has been kindled against us, because our fathers did not obey the words of this scroll to do all that has been prescribed for us." Josiah went on to carry out a general religious reform, purging his realm of idol worship and reestablishing religious practices (like the Passover sacrifice) that had been abandoned (II Kings 22–23). Many scholars think that the scroll that caused such a commotion was the Book of Deuteronomy (and some say the "reformers" had it written and "found" for the occasion). In any case, now, as then, archaeology is not just a dry academic discipline, but rather an activity that seems inseparable from current religious and ideological discourse.

Archaeology is an important component of modern Israeli culture. Some have called it our national sport; others see it as a kind of secular religion. I would estimate that an archaeological find — or controversy — makes it to the front page of the daily paper at least once a month. It's hard to imagine a family vacation or an annual school trip that does not include at least one site. The whole national park system is supported by the income from admission fees to the Masada excavations. A number of archaeologists have become celebrities, like Yigal Yadin, the army chief of staff who went on to lead the excavations at Masada. Perhaps the most famous amateur archaeologist — and owner of one of the largest illegal collections of artifacts — was Moshe Dayan, who was nearly killed in the collapse of a structure he was excavating. Archaeological controversies can become strident academic and public debates — like the one currently raging over whether the archaeological evidence supports the biblical account of the kingdoms of David and Solomon.

Nelson Glueck (1900–1971), a Reform rabbi, former president of Hebrew Union College-Jewish Institute of Religion, and a passionate Zionist, was one of the leading archaeologists of his generation. He was a classic example of the type of archaeologist who walked the land with a Bible in hand, seeking the rocks that matched and verified the text. This approach has become somewhat controversial: We are supposed to look at the physical evidence without preconceived expectations based on the text.

Why this fascination with archaeology? Because Jews are obsessed with the past? Because we simply encounter remains of ancient life everywhere we turn? Because our insecurity drives us to prove to ourselves and others that we really do have roots here, deep in history? Because in reforging Jewish identity as secular nationalism, we needed to find an authentic, geographically based past that was independent of exile-based religion? All of the above? Interestingly, we are not alone in our digging for connections with the past in the soil of our homeland; other modern nation-states, like Greece and Turkey and Egypt, have worked hard to discover the links between their glorious ancient cultures and present-day reality.

And dig as we do to find our roots, others are digging to find different roots in the same soil: A couple of years ago an Arab friend mentioned that he had volunteered for a year to work on the excavations under Al-Aqsa Mosque in Jerusalem, carried out by the Wakf, the Muslim religious trust. "And I learned something very interesting," he said. "It turns out that there is no evidence of any Jewish occupation or building on that mountain [the Temple Mount]!"

I guess we'd better keep our shovels dry; we can't afford to stop digging.

60. . . . And a Happy New Year *(January 2, 2005)*

I accompanied a group of Israeli teachers on a Partnership 2000 (a Jewish Agency program that pairs Israeli and Diaspora communities) visit to meet their peers in an American Jewish community last week. One of the teachers went shopping with her hostess for school materials, and found some great bulletin-board borders. "But you can't buy those," said her hostess. "Those are Christmas symbols!" To which the Israeli responded, "But to us they have no meaning;

they are pretty and colorful and don't have any symbolic overtones to my students." Their argument became the subject of a discussion among the whole group, which made clear to the Israelis that the colorful, cheerful, happy "holiday season" feels to many Jews and Jewish educators like a powerful flood that threatens to wash away their own sense of who they (or their students) are. Interestingly, this is not a new dilemma:

> R. Gamaliel was bathing in the bath of Aphrodite in Akko (Acre). Proklos ben Philosophos [a non-Jew] asked him: It is written in your Torah, "Let nothing forbidden stick to your hand" [Deuteronomy 13:18]—so why are you bathing in the bath of Aphrodite [Venus]? He said to him: One must not answer in the bathhouse. When he went out, he answered: I didn't come into her space, she came into mine: One doesn't say, "Let's build a bathhouse in honor of Aphrodite," but rather, "Let's make an Aphrodite to decorate our bathhouse." (*Mishnah Avodah Zarah* 3:4)

Rabban Gamaliel II, the *Nasi,* or the head of the Sanhedrin, the rabbinical leader of the Jewish people in Israel in the first century, sees the statue of the pagan goddess adorning the local health club as merely a decoration, with no religious symbolism. Even his non-Jewish fellow bather is surprised by his position. On the other hand, we know of Rabbis who refused even to look at a coin that had the image of the emperor on them, not wanting to give the appearance of showing respect for a graven image. So the question of when a symbol loses its meaning is never simple.

For most nonreligious Israelis, Christmas and especially New Year's Day are simply universal Western observances without religious meaning; and since Christians only make up 2 percent of the population here, we are not exactly under pressure to adopt

Christian practices, or in danger of losing our Jewish identity. Today I noticed a poster advertising a Christmas disco party at a nearby kibbutz pub. And New Year's Eve parties have been big business here for years, just as they are in the rest of the West. It is not called New Year's, though, but rather Sylvester, which ironically brings the problem to the surface: December 31 is St. Sylvester's Day in the Roman Catholic calendar of saints. Pope Sylvester I lived in the fourth century—it is said that he baptized the emperor Constantine. In Germany, his day was traditionally celebrated with music and dance, food and drink, at a Sylvester Ball. Until the rise of secular society in the past two hundred years, the *civil new year* was probably not a term with any meaning: The night of December 31 was indeed a religious holiday in Christian Europe (note that January 1 would be the day of Jesus's brit milah, too). Not many Jews in the Middle Ages were wondering if it was OK to celebrate.

The fact that the day is called Sylvester here is an attempt to remind us of its origins. Thus, for example, in some years and some cities, the rabbinate has threatened to revoke the kashrut license of any restaurant hosting a Sylvester party, which to most Israelis sounds absurd. Who gets to decide the meaning of a symbol? What about Halloween in American Jewish schools? Is there anybody in America for whom Halloween is a religious holiday—aside from the Jews who make a point of not celebrating it because it is a pagan religious holiday? But if Halloween is OK, then what about St. Valentine's Day? And what about candy canes and colored lights and even a December holiday tree? It's a slippery slope, and even in Israel we can lose our footing.

61. Hebrew *(March 13, 2005)*

Suddenly Rachel climbed up and stretched out on the trunk of a carob up on the top of a hill. From there . . . she raised her voice high in song toward us, the group down in the *wadi*. We heard . . . not only her voice but a powerful echo responding: The whole landscape sang in ancient Sefardi Hebrew, which seemed to have been preserved here in its purity. It was as if our far-off ancestors, shepherds and maidens of Israel, who went out into these mountains on some day of joy or mourning, had hidden those beautifully authentic, precisely articulated Hebrew sounds in the crevices of the rocks to be preserved there till the day of deliverance came. And the day was now beginning to come.

—Zalman Shazar, *Morning Stars*
(The Jewish Publication Society of America, 1967)

There is no question that for me, an important element of my Jewish identity is Hebrew. I don't know why. I only know that I love the language—its grammar, its word families, the associations it supports between the biblical and the modern experience. I love hearing it spoken well, in a lecture, in a play, on a bus. And while the intrusion of English often annoys me, I remind myself that there is no such thing as a pure language, and that classical Hebrew is full of words absorbed from Greek, Persian, and other languages, at various points in our history. I tend to resist romantic nationalistic tendencies in Zionism; however, I have a soft spot for the place of Hebrew in Zionism. I see the revival of spoken Hebrew, the creation of a whole national culture in the course of a century, as one of the central achievements of the Zionist enterprise.

If we understand Zionism as an attempt to secularize Jewish identity, to create a way to be Jewish even if you don't believe in God and God's commandments, to transform Jewish identity from religious to cultural/national, then the establishment of Hebrew as a modern spoken language was a huge success. Until Zionism, Hebrew for most Diaspora Jews was the language of prayer and Torah study; they lived their secular lives in

Yiddish, English, Arabic, Ladino, or some other language. Now there are millions of Jews who neither pray nor study Torah, yet live their entire lives in Hebrew. Their Jewish identity has been transformed entirely. Whether this is a perversion of Judaism or its elevation to a higher level is an interesting and difficult question. On the one hand, if you believe that the core of Judaism is faith and mitzvot (whether you are Orthodox, Conservative, Reform, or Reconstructionist), then this total secularization represents a catastrophe. On the other hand, no matter how rich and sophisticated our translations of traditional texts into English or other languages, only Hebrew speakers have total access to the deepest meanings of those texts in their authentic original. Even the most secular Israeli has the option of getting inside the Bible in a way that even the most spiritually intense reader of translations cannot.

One of the early players in the development of the education system in modern *Eretz Yisrael* was the *Hilfsverein*, a German-Jewish philanthropic organization that ran the first teachers' seminary in Palestine in the early years of the twentieth century. It was the *Hilfsverein* that opened the Technion in 1914. To their leadership, it was unthinkable that a technical college could function in any language other than German. The students at the teachers' seminary and some of their teachers went on strike to protest, in what became known as the Language War. In the end, the *Hilfsverein* capitulated—even though there were no appropriate books in Hebrew, nor had much of the relevant vocabulary even been invented yet. The point was that language is the substrate of culture, it is a central element of our identity; it is, in a way, what Zionism is all about. Schools conducted in another language would cripple the Zionist vision from the start.

I think it is unfortunate that we so often reduce Zionism to identification with the state as a political entity, losing touch with the deep and powerful impact of the movement on the very nature of Jewish identity in our time—expressed and symbolized by the revitalization of the Hebrew language.

62. Play It Again . . . Naomi Shemer
(August 7, 2005)

All of these, all of these—
Please watch over them for me, my God.
The honey and the sting,
The bitter and the sweet.
Don't uproot what has been planted,
Don't forget the hope.
Return me and I shall return
To the good land.

—Naomi Shemer

Touring the Galilee with American Jewish teachers, I visited the Kinneret cemetery for the first time in several years. This beautiful, serene spot near the southern tip of the Sea of Galilee is a kind of informal national shrine; by reading the epitaphs there, one can learn a great deal about the history of Zionism and Israel. Not only are famous leaders and thinkers buried there, but nameless infants from the early 1900s, anonymous refugees, pioneers, poets—not just private memories, but national ones as well. Perhaps the main reason that Israelis make pilgrimages to this spot is the grave of Rachel Bluwstein, the unofficial poet laureate of the *Yishuv* (the Jewish settlement in Israel before 1948). She tried her hand at pioneering, then went to work with refugee children in Russia after the First World War, where she caught tuberculosis and was not allowed to return to the kibbutz. She lived out the rest of her short life in Tel Aviv; her poems were published regularly in the daily newspapers and were hugely popular in the 1920s. Many were set to music and have achieved the status of folk songs. There is a compartment attached to her gravestone containing a very dog-eared book of her collected poems (fastened to a chain). A recurring theme in her poems is her attachment to the land—to this land around the Kinneret—in a tone not of militant nationalism but of sad longing and personal rootedness.

This summer there was a new grave in the cemetery—that of Naomi Shemer. Her songs, too, were central to the popular culture of Israel for two generations, and many, like Rachel's, have become folk songs. She was a secular Zionist, but her songs are rich in references to traditional terms and concepts. For example, in the stanza above, you can see the references to Ecclesiastes 3:2 and Jeremiah 31:17—and probably others. That makes them great tools for Jewish educators abroad; here in Israel I suspect that many, if not most, of the people singing her songs miss many of her allusions. For example, I don't think many Israelis educated in the state's secular schools catch the connection between the "Jerusalem of Gold" they know by heart and the "Jerusalem of gold" wedding ring R. Akiba gave his wife, according to the Babylonian Talmud (*Shabbat* 59a–b).

But then, Naomi Shemer didn't know that "Jerusalem of Gold" would become the anthem of the Six-Day War—nor that her Hebrew version of the Beatles' "Let It Be" would become the anthem of the Yom Kippur War—nor that the song quoted above would become an anthem of the settlers removed from Sinai in 1982 and from Gaza in 2005. She had an amazing ability to write in a language and a musical idiom that really spoke to the masses; her songs can be seen, in a remarkable number of cases, as part of the liturgy of secular Zionist religion.

In the face of the McDonaldization of Israel, it is comforting to know that there is a strong and continuing strand of true cultural creativity here; Naomi Shemer, whose career spanned the transition from the days of the folk-dancing pioneers to the days of the high-tech entrepreneurs in the global economy, was herself both a pioneer and an entrepreneur—and a cultural icon. It was her life's work and lasting achievement to facilitate a successful encounter between the language of the Jewish past and the experience of the Jewish present, thus providing a basis for a Jewish future.

63. Comfort Food *(July 27, 2008)*

When you have eaten your fill, give thanks to the Eternal your God for the good land given to you.

—Deuteronomy 8:10

So there I was, in the business district of a sleepy development town on a hot summer day at 1:00 P.M., with my scheduled meeting with a local school principal suddenly delayed for half an hour. The heat, the dingy surroundings, the cracked sidewalks, the number of people sitting around on the steps and on the chairs in front of the kiosks with nothing to do—the setting was somehow familiar, a depressing slice of a certain aspect of Israeli culture that seems not to have changed in sixty years, and can still be encountered in small towns like this one scattered through the landscape from the northern border to the heart of the Negev. The scene seemed lifted directly from *Turn Left at the End of the World* or *The Band's Visit* (two recent Israeli films set in development towns).

One could see the half hour I was destined to spend there as a dismal prospect—or as an opportunity; I was hungry, and it was lunchtime, so I chose to see it as an opportunity, confident that I would find a falafel stand nearby. Sure enough, there it was, and the tables were all occupied, with a line at the counter, suggesting that the falafel would be freshly made. The pita was soft, the falafel balls hot and lightly crispy. This place had a nice palette of salads, all the "regulars": fine-cut cucumbers and tomatoes, fresh green cabbage and red cabbage and sauerkraut, marinated hot peppers and sweet peppers, finely sliced onion seasoned with sumac, fried eggplant strips, pickled baby eggplants swimming in bright purple brine, sliced pickles and bitter olives and hot sauce, and, of course, a squeeze bottle of diluted techina. Falafel may be the national fast food, but every eater gets to make his or her own individual version; you have to answer quickly as the vendor's tongs hover briefly over each section of the salad table. I happily settled down at a shared table with my falafel, a plastic cup of olives, and a sweet grapefruit drink. I would say I enjoyed people-watching, but eating a falafel successfully requires concentration: To avoid dripping techina down your shirt, to prevent stray components from falling out, and to ensure that you maximize the mixture of tastes and don't get left with three plain falafel balls in dry pita, you must plan the geometry of your attack and constantly recalculate the angle of the next bite. It was delicious, and I was grateful to the principal for letting me know he would be half an hour late for our appointment.

This little gastronomic interlude brought back a long string of memories, of similar meals eaten in similar surroundings, central bus stations and downtowns in Kiriat Shmona and Safed, Beersheba and Dimona, Acre, and Afula. In my first stay in Israel as a high school student, falafel was a staple part of a trip down to the Hadar or the port in Haifa. And subsequently it remained the treat I allowed myself when traveling the country for work or pleasure. When I did our weekly shopping at Machaneh Yehuda market in Jerusalem, my compensation to myself for carrying the heavy baskets in the heat or the rain was falafel at Blondie's. Falafel stands have become fewer over the years. First there was the Great Pizza Invasion of the early '70s, and then McDonald's and KFC, and now the wave of boutique sandwich shops with their avocado and goat cheese and multigrain bread. Recently, my daughter and I decided to go out for falafel on a Saturday night near her apartment in Ramat Aviv, an upscale neighborhood near Tel Aviv University. No luck; we had to settle for pizza.

There is something about falafel: Spicy, nutritious, cheap—it seems to taste the best when you buy and eat it in the most unpretentious surroundings, a sort of proletarian comfort food that keeps us connected to a simpler time.

64. Chickpeas *(August 14, 2005)*

Ruth follows her mother-in-law, Naomi, back to Israel from Moab when they have both become widowed. Naomi sends Ruth out to glean from the fields of a distant relative, Boaz. Romance is in the offing. Indeed, Boaz notices her and suggests they do lunch:

> At mealtime, Boaz said to her, "Come over here and partake of the meal, and dip your morsel in vinegar." (Ruth 2:14)

The popular Israeli novelist and columnist Meir Shalev, in his series of lectures and essays giving a modern, secular interpretation to the Bible, argues that *vinegar* is a mistranslation. The Hebrew word *chameitz* is indeed from the root referring to fermentation or souring (*chameitz* means "leavened bread," *chamutzim* means "pickles"), and in modern Hebrew means "vinegar"; but Shalev insists it is related to the Arabic *chumus*, or "chickpeas." If so, then the luncheon menu of Boaz's workers was not bread in vinegar, but bread in chumus, which makes, I suppose, a lot more sense (at least to my taste).

Among the older generation of tourists to Israel, first-time visitors seem surprised not to find plentiful bagels—or corned beef; after all, if this is a Jewish state, how can it not serve Jewish food? For those a little more sophisticated, it used to be that falafel symbolized Israeli food. Now, every group I meet seems obsessed with *shawarma* (gyros), traditionally made from lamb, though usually made today from turkey. I'm with Meir Shalev—for me, the quintessential Israeli food is chumus. It is totally ubiquitous—in the simplest fast food joints and in the fanciest restaurants. It is served as part of the standard appetizer salad bar and as a main course, plain and with a whole range of additions, from beans to pine nuts to meat. Nowadays the variety of brands and flavors of prepared chumus fills a whole section of the supermarket refrigerator case. It is cheap, nourishing, relatively easy to make, and the perfect sandwich filling or dip. Probably the three most common lunch-box or picnic sandwiches in Israel are chumus, yellow cheese, and chocolate spread (though chocolate spread pretty much drops out of the running once you graduate from the army). Only Americans eat peanut butter and jelly.

As an ingathering of immigrants from every corner of the world (and foreign workers), Israel indeed offers bagels and corned beef, Thai and French delicacies, Moroccan couscous, Italian pizza, Russian sausages and Ethiopian bread, Argentinian steaks—and, of course, McDonald's and KFC. You really can get anything you want. So what is Israeli food? Interestingly, none of these Jewish or global imports has really assimilated. Israeli food is regional food, Palestinian food: chumus, falafel, *shawarma*. Our comfort foods are the foods we found here, not the ones we brought with us.

I'm not sure this is intuitively obvious, nor trivial. It raises some interesting questions: How much of Israeli culture is Jewish culture? How much of who we are is where we live? In rebelling against the culture of the Diaspora and seeking to create our own, authentic Jewish culture, we revived our own ancient language; we created a new literature and art, anchored in the past by historical themes and textual allusions; we set our traditional texts to modern music—and wrote and composed folk songs that reflected our experience in returning to our land. But what about food? On holidays we eat the foods we ate in the Diaspora—they link us to our roots in a Jewish tradition filtered through the Diaspora experience. But on weekdays we eat the foods of the land and of the people of the land. Maybe we like chumus so much not only because it is tasty, cheap, and nourishing, but because by making it ours, we affirm how much we belong to this place.

65. Manners *(August 28, 2005)*

I remember that when I first visited Israel, as a teenager, one of the things that made a strong impression on me was the sign at the front of every car in the Haifa subway (the Carmelit), consisting of the first phrase of Leviticus 19:32:

> You shall rise before the aged [and the verse continues: "and show deference to the old; you shall fear your God: I am the Eternal"].

To me that sign symbolized the best in—and what was distinctive about—Israeli culture: a biblical verse being used to make a value statement in a totally secular and mundane setting. In other words, someone in Haifa's Transportation Department had seen fit to immortalize in stenciled paint the connection between a classical text and civilized behavior on the subway. That's what we came back here for, isn't it—the revitalization of the tradition? Later, Egged (the largest intercity bus company) picked up on the idea, and such signs can now be seen in many buses all over the country.

However, the warm, fuzzy feelings that I get from such examples of Israeli culture are often severely cooled by the experience of trying to board that same bus on a Sunday morning. If you mention to an Israeli—or to a tourist—the Israeli attitude toward waiting in line, you will get something between an ironic chuckle and a furious expletive. Everybody knows—and everybody suffers from and hates—the unfathomable reality of Israeli line behavior. Unfortunately, this has a corollary in driving behavior, where the stakes are, unfortunately, a lot higher. Much has been written about this favorite "only in Israel" topic, and a range of explanations proposed.

Among them: The tension of being always at war; the memories of shortages; the rebellion against the lines of communist Russia; the Third World; the heat; the melting pot; the mutual suspicions and mistrust of an immigrant society; the valuing of total honesty (niceness is nothing more than a form of insincerity); lack of "culture." I have given up trying to understand it, and have made pretty major progress in talking myself out of the rage that I feel when I arrive first to an empty bus stop and then find myself missing the bus when the doors close in my face, fifty people having pushed their way in front of me — or when the highway is reduced from two lanes to one and no one — no one — will hesitate for a second to let me merge in front of him. The method is clear: Never make eye contact and look straight ahead as if there were no one else on the road or trying to squeeze in the door — eye contact would obligate you to take the other person's existence into account and maybe even recognize her claim to the right of passage, which, of course, is unacceptable. People who let others get ahead of them are called *friars* in Israeli slang — usually translated as "suckers." "Why should I be a *friar*?" seems like a kind of national motto.

This seemingly trivial cultural phenomenon is one of the most frustrating and disappointing aspects of life here for immigrants from the lands of long, orderly lines and "Have a nice day." It can truly test — or overwhelm — a person's sense of humor. And I think the frustration is intensified by the conflict between the reality and the ideal — between the crude pushiness of Israeli society (from the bus stop to the Knesset) and our vision of a state founded on values like "You shall rise before the aged," "You shall not . . . bear a grudge," "Love your neighbor as yourself . . ." and "You shall not wrong [a stranger]" (all from Leviticus 19). Once again, I find myself faced with the temptation to be swept along in the current, and to accept the reality—instead of trying to stand firm and be a model of commitment to the ideal. It is easy to simply outpush the others (after all, I do need to get on a bus, eventually); but then—what will become of us? I have a friend, a creative and outspoken teacher, who made buttons for herself and her students, reading: "I'm a *friar*—and proud of it!"

I'm a *friar*—and proud of it.

66. Dust to Dust *(September 28, 2008)*

> ... till you return to the earth—that earth you were taken from; for dust you are, and to dust you shall return.
>
> —Genesis 3:19

Avraham Buxdorf died last week. Avraham and Zina made *aliyah* from Moldava with their extended family around 1990, when they were about sixty—at the peak of the wave of Russian *aliyah* (and right around the time my family came from the United States). He had worked as a driver in the old country. Indeed, he actually arrived in Israel with his Lada and kept it running for a number of years. (There were many jokes about Ladas—like the one about the guy who filled the Lada's gas tank and thus doubled the value of his car. Today, at $8 a gallon, that is less funny). They settled in Karmiel, and early on found work here at Shorashim in our seminar center. Both Avraham and Zina—and at times one of their sons, and Avraham's sister, and her daughter, and the teenagers of the next generation—did housekeeping, laundry, repairs, deliveries, dishwashing, waiting—all the support tasks involved in operating a youth hostel. They were also much in demand by the residents of Shorashim for child care, house-sitting, and the like. Avraham was a big, barrel-chested, bear of a man. He never mastered much Hebrew, getting by in Yiddish, Russian, and with Zina's help. He kept working hard, despite his age and illnesses (heart disease, throat cancer). We saw less of them after we closed the hostel in 2003; indeed, many people in Shorashim didn't even know that in 2006 they had won a green card lottery, and, traumatized by the impact of the war in Karmiel, departed for Brooklyn, where Avraham's cancer recurred and ultimately took his life.

It seems that Zina, who does not plan to return to stay in Israel, decided that Avraham should be buried here, and brought his body back. Many of us attended the funeral. Waiting for it to start, a number of us talked among ourselves in English. Everyone else was speaking Russian. Karmiel, a town of 50,000, has one cemetery that is typical of Israeli municipal cemeteries. It is located at the end of the industrial zone, surrounded by a shopping mall parking lot, an aluminum extrusion factory, and a ready-mix cement silo complex. The ground is coarse limestone gravel. Graves are side by side in long rows. There is no room for greenery; there is no shade except for a canopy over the eulogy area—a stone slab in the center of a plaza near the entrance. Since there are no funeral homes in Israel, the entire funeral generally takes place at the cemetery—the body is placed on the slab, the mourners stand around it, and eulogies and Psalms are recited there before the crowd follows the body to the gravesite. The *chevrah kadisha* (burial society) is part of the religious bureaucracy, and takes care of all arrangements. In this case, there was no rabbi and no eulogy. The body was brought in on a cart (in a shroud, covered with a velvet blanket—no casket), we all gathered around, and a member of the *chevrah kadisha*, wearing a plaid shirt and a baseball cap, recited some Psalms from a laminated notebook and helped the sons recite *Kaddish;* he then led the way to the grave. The rocky earth had been put in plastic garbage cans, which made it relatively easy to fill the grave quickly by just dumping them in. Then the many people who had brought bouquets and wreaths piled them on the grave. Few of those present had much knowledge of traditional practices; the custom of lining up and paying respects to the family as they leave the cemetery was skipped; people drifted away.

Interestingly, one can find beautiful, green cemeteries in Israel—generally on kibbutzim and other small communities for whom the aesthetic element is a value. However, urban cemeteries share the same desolate, industrial atmosphere we found in Karmiel. On the one hand, there is something to be said for cemeteries being pleasant places to visit. On the other hand, maybe there is also something to be said for letting death be death, harsh and final, without trying to soften it, disguise it, euphemize it. No casket, no limousine, no perpetual care. Just dust.

PART VIII

The Land Itself

67. Rain *(December 10, 2000)*

I will grant the rain for your land in season, the early rain and the late. You shall gather in your new grain and wine and oil—I will also provide grass in the fields for your cattle—and thus you shall eat your fill. Take care not to be lured away to serve other gods and bow to them. For the Eternal's anger will flare up against you, shutting up the skies so that there will be no rain and the ground will not yield its produce . . .

—Deuteronomy 11:14–17

After a week of threatening forecasts, we finally had a rainy day yesterday. It feels so good!

As summer wears on into fall, the color drains out of the landscape, so that mountain and valley, horizon and sky, trees and roads all are seen through a filter of grayish-brown. Distant vistas of mountain and sea are flat and colorless, like a washed-out old photograph.

Then come the first rains (usually during Sukkot), and by December, the dust is washed away and you can see forever. On my morning walk around the moshav with the dogs, I am struck by the vibrant colors that surround me: a lush green carpet of new growth of weeds/wildflowers, the natural brush and young Jewish National Fund pine trees in a whole palette of greens and browns, tiny pink early crocuses against the brown soil, billowing white clouds against a pure blue sky. The air is washed so clear that I can see the ships in Haifa Bay. The rain brings a powerful feeling of renewal, of rebirth. I find it fascinating how I respond emotionally, spiritually, to such a simple, routine natural phenomenon. I suppose it is no different from the feelings I used to have on a crisp fall day in Chicago, or on one of those early spring days when the sun was warm and crocuses peeked through melting snow. The transitions of the seasons seem to set off feelings of transition, of renewal, in our hearts. Despite all our efforts to distance ourselves from nature, to control it, to protect ourselves from its vagaries, we still vibrate to its rhythms.

Here, though, I think the vibration might be stronger because the dependency is clearer. Even though I am not a farmer, I know that rain is life and drought is death. As the fall burns on, I find myself thirsty for that first rain, watching for it, sniffing for it. And when it comes, what a feeling of relief, of joy! No wonder that the ancient Canaanites worshiped Baal, god of thunderstorms. No wonder that the prophets and the psalmist use the image of water as an image of life. No wonder that the prayer for rain at Shemini Atzeret seems so right, so genuine, so authentic.

Israel, with its high-tech economy and its export of sophisticated irrigation systems to the whole world, has not gained control over Baal. We are at the mercy of the weather, no less than were our ancient ancestors. The newspapers anxiously chronicle the rising and falling of the water level in Lake Kinneret (the Sea of Galilee), the national reservoir, as it fills (in a good year) during the winter and empties during the summer. When things get really bad during the summer, the government even runs public service announcements urging us to conserve water. There is a dissonance here: We always took pride in Israel's image as an "old-new" land, combining love of ancient landscape with the most modern sophistication in agriculture, afforestation, preservation; and yet we seem helpless to create a culture of conservation, to in any way release ourselves from total dependency on the annual rainfall statistics. Each summer the papers are full of doomsday prophecies and discussions of depleted aquifers, of oil tankers filled with imported water from Turkey, of emergency desalination plant construction . . . and then—it rains! And we go back to washing our cars and watering crops that we have no business growing in a semiarid climate.

On the other hand, I wonder if part of what attracts me to Israel is that sense of dependency, the inability to escape the awareness that for all our sophistication, we are at the mercy of the elements, that we are not omnipotent. If we do someday get our act together to build a rational water economy in this country, will the first rain of the season still stir up those same deep feelings? Is there not perhaps something authentic, human, and spiritually significant about feeling exposed to the rhythms of nature and dependent on them year in and year out? One of the things I most love about living in Israel is the experience of the correlation between the Jewish calendar and the agricultural cycle of the land. Just as I find it somehow gratifying to know that when I see the full moon it is the fifteenth of the Hebrew month, I also feel good when I see the seasonal rhythm of the land echoed in the calendar of holidays. There is in this correspondence the naturalness, the rootedness, the harmony that Zionism sought— and found. The question is, Will we be able to hold on to it?

68. Walkabout *(January 15, 2006)*

When Saul returned from pursuing the Philistines, he was told that David was in the wilderness of En-gedi. So Saul took three thousand picked men from all Israel and went in search of David and his men in the direction of the rocks of the wild goats.

—I Samuel 24:2–3

Winter having finally set in with a vengeance, with continuous damp cold punctuated by howling hailstorms, Tami and I decided it was time for some desert therapy. So we reserved a long weekend with some friends at the kibbutz hotel at Ein Gedi, on the shore of the Dead Sea. We drove through gray drizzle for the first two and a half hours, as far as Jerusalem; but then, as we descended to the Judean Desert, the sky cleared, and we could drive with the windows open. After dinner, we hung up our winter coats and joined a moonlight tour of the kibbutz botanical garden. Ein Gedi sits at the foot of desolate, craggy cliffs that rise from the shore of the Dead Sea, at the outflow of two adjacent canyons through which flow streams fed by springs of fresh water; it is a classic oasis. The kibbutz, in the fifty years since its founding, has exploited its unique climate and water supply to create a truly breathtaking environment (recognized by UNESCO as a world-class botanical garden), where desert and rain forest species grow side by side in weird and lush profusion, throughout the public spaces as well as around the members' houses and the hotel.

The next day we hiked the Arugot Canyon, along the modest stream that cascades through the strikingly eroded rock formations. It was a Friday, and ours was the only car in the parking lot. Twice we encountered, close-up, herds of ibex, the indigenous wild goats with their beards and oversized curving horns, foraging for bits of vegetation along the cliffs above the canyon. There wasn't much other wildlife in evidence—caravans of ants and a large crab sidling across the path, blending perfectly with the pinkish-tan of the rocks. And I noticed a number of openings that seemed likely to be the burrows of some animal, but there were spiderwebs across their entrances.

According to a midrash in the medieval collection *The Alphabet of Ben Sira*, the future King David once noticed a spider in his garden and questioned God: What is the point of having such a creature in Your world? It spends its life weaving, but never yields any cloth. Later, when David was hiding from Saul in a cave in the desert of

Ein Gedi, Saul's men approached the cave and were about to enter in search of David, but a spider had woven its web across the entrance after David had gone inside; Saul noticed the web and concluded that there was no point in searching the cave, as it was obvious that no one could have entered recently. Saved by the spider he had disparaged, David thus received the answer to his challenge to God, and was moved to exclaim (Psalm 104:24): O Lord, how many are Your works! In wisdom have You made them all!

It is amazing how you can drive just a few hours in this country and arrive in a totally different landscape and climate. It is even more amazing how you can drive just a few hours and find yourself in a different millennium, walking around the stage of a tragic drama that was played out here three thousand years ago. The wild goats are still here. So are the spiders. So are the stories. So are we.

69. Rabbi Yose's Silence *(May 28, 2006)*

Moving into summer and the peak of tourist season, I find myself leading study tours at Zippori again, about once a week. This is one of my favorite sites in Israel, and I have been following its development—as an excavation and as a tourist site—since it opened in the early '90s. The combination of the physical beauty of the site, with its striking panoramic view of the whole Galilee; the well-preserved ruins and beautiful mosaics, of which more are uncovered every year; and the many correlations between archaeological findings and rabbinic texts make it possible for me to visit Zippori over and over without it ever becoming stale for me.

Perhaps even more important than these considerations in making Zippori attractive and interesting is the site's ability to stimulate thinking and discussion of dilemmas that are as alive today as they were two millennia ago. For example, in Tractate *Shabbat* of the Babylonian Talmud (33b), we find this story:

Once R. Yehuda and R. Yose and R. Shimon were sitting
with Yehuda the Convert. R. Yehuda said: How wonderful are the works of this people [the Romans]! They have
established markets, they have built bridges, they have
built baths. R. Yose was silent. R. Shimon bar Yochai
answered: They established markets—for prostitutes to
work there; they built bridges—in order to collect tolls;
they built baths—to pamper themselves. Yehuda the Convert went and repeated their words and the authorities
heard, who said: Yehuda who exalted—will be exalted;
Yose who was silent—will be exiled to Zippori; Shimon
who condemned—will be killed.

The debate between the two extreme positions—Rabbi Yehuda,
who emphasizes the benefits of Roman rule for our quality of life,
and Rabbi Shimon, who sees the moral price that such benefits exact—can easily be translated into modern terms, as we debate the
benefits and costs of globalization. Specifically, here in Israel, there
is no question that these two positions regarding Rome resonate
strongly in the debate over American cultural influence. Clearly, on
the level of physical comfort, free exchange of information, richness of choices of what to wear and what to eat, what to read and
where to travel, Israel has benefited greatly from the penetration
of global capitalism and American consumer culture. A generation
ago this was a very provincial place; visiting relatives were encouraged to bring tuna fish, coffee, and videotapes. The wait for instal-
lation of a phone line was several months, and the token-operated
pay phones often didn't work. On a hot day you welcomed the
long line at the bank, because it gave you plenty of time to enjoy
the air-conditioning. Everyday life was simpler, and more difficult.
Everything took longer, took more effort, with more discomfort.
Coming from America, you made fun of Israeli inconveniences and
primitiveness (on a good day) or cursed it (on a bad day)—but you

also had the feeling that this life had a certain inexplicable authenticity: The suffering made you feel righteous. In living here, you were paying a price for an ideal, which, annoying and frustrating as it was, felt good.

Now, of course, most of these discomforts and annoyances are quaint memories. Israel has one of the highest per capita rates of cell-phone ownership in the world. No one imports tuna fish or coffee in her suitcase any more. Air-conditioned malls have replaced the downtown shopping experience. We have Pizza Hut, Toys "R" Us, and Office Depot. So if life is so good, is the nostalgia for those good old uncomfortable days just nostalgia, or has something of value actually been lost in the transition? Could it be that, as Rabbi Shimon suggested, hidden within all this comfort and convenience and sophistication lie destructive forces of selfishness and alienation, a numbing of moral sensitivity, and a weakening of social solidarity? Should we welcome progress, like Rabbi Yehuda, or fight it at all costs, like Rabbi Shimon? Or is the best we can hope for to be Rabbi Yose, struggling (in my imagination, at least) in silence with his ambivalence?

70. A Fault Line Runs Through It *(July 25, 2004)*

Recently, I was standing in the living room talking to Tami, who was sitting on the couch, when suddenly she said, "There, did you feel something?" I had to admit that I didn't know what she was talking about. Sure enough, the next day we read in the newspaper about a minor earthquake that had affected the region. This is not the first time Tami has been aware of seismic activity under our feet, while I have remained oblivious to it. The point here is not my insensitivity, but rather, the fact that we live in an earthquake zone. Sometimes I wonder what God was thinking when He chose this particular sliver of the world to promise to us. OK, so our desert may not be quite as arid and forbidding as that of our neighbors to the east and the west—but it also doesn't lie on top of vast deposits of petroleum, as their deserts do. Nicely positioned as a bridge between Asia and Africa—and between the Mediterranean Sea and the Indian Ocean—this land has always served as a crossroads for trade and cultural transmission—but also for the conquering armies of competing empires, who have been marching back and forth across our little patch of homeland since history began to be recorded. A land flowing with milk and honey indeed, but only in a rainy year; living as we do squeezed between the Mediterranean and the desert, it rains only during half the year, and the entire cycle of natural flora and agriculture depends on how many millimeters of rain fall during the winter months.

Droughts, wars, energy prices—we can deal with it. But whose idea was it to settle directly along one of the most active fault lines in the world? From Metulla in the north to Eilat in the south, the dominant feature of the landscape of Israel is the Syro-African rift valley, a massive meeting of tectonic plates that lies beneath the Jordan River, the Sea of Galilee, the Dead Sea, the Arava, and the Gulf of Aqaba. It is this fault that gives us hot springs and sulfur springs—and tar springs beneath the Dead Sea. And it is the shifting of plates in this valley that has produced a long series of earthquakes—seismologists estimate about one every fifty years.

> The words of Amos, a sheep breeder from Tekoa, who prophesied concerning Israel in the reigns of Kings Uzziah of Judah and Jeroboam, son of Joash of Israel, two years before the earthquake. (Amos 1:1)

> And the valley of the hills shall be stopped up . . . as it was stopped up as a result of the earthquake in the days of King Uzziah of Judah. (Zechariah 14:5)

After the quake in Uzziah's reign, in 759 B.C.E., we know of a number of other major ones: in 31 B.C.E., 68 C.E., 553, 746 (destroying Bet Shean), 963, 1033, 1067, 1138, 1202, 1546, 1759 (destroying Safed), 1837 (Safed again), and 1927 (four hundred deaths in Tiberias). The most recent that caused property damage was in 1995; even I felt that one. If you were looking for reasons not to visit, now you have another one.

Like everyone else, it seems that our connection to place is not based on rational considerations. If people chose their location rationally, think of all the places that would be uninhabited today—places prone to killer hurricanes, floods, earthquakes, droughts, blizzards, terror, and violent crime. We are bound to places by memory, by history, by inertia, by ideology, by the joy of the spring after the blizzard, the calm after the earthquake. Place becomes part of our identity and it is nearly impossible to tear it out of us. There is a deep insight into human nature in the account of the first earthquake, at Sodom (right on the fault line). The angels said to Lot's family: "Flee for your life! Do not look behind you" (Genesis 19:17). But "Lot's wife looked back, and she thereupon turned into a pillar of salt" (Genesis 19:26). And if you don't believe it, you can see the pillar of salt by the shore of the Dead Sea, to this day. Meanwhile, here we sit, occupied with our trivial pursuit of peace and prosperity, waiting for the Big One.

71. The Center of the World *(September 19, 2004)*

Among the holidays, Rosh HaShanah and Yom Kippur are unique in their focus on the inner life of the individual. The pilgrimage festivals are rich in links to nature and to the Land of Israel, full of colorful symbols and practices. Purim and Chanukah deal with historical events in the life of the nation. Shabbat is a major building block of community. The High Holy Days, on the other hand, are days of introspection, of personal spiritual activity, emphasizing each person's own relationship to God. We gather as a community, and many of the prayers are phrased in national terms, but the liturgy—and the spirit of the days—leads to an experience that is very personal, inward, introspective. And because of this personal emphasis, these days seem perhaps the least "national," the least bound to any particular location. Wherever we are, we can perform the three key acts of the season: praying, repenting, and giving *tzedakah*.

Interestingly, though, the traditional liturgy for Yom Kippur is extremely place-centered. Leviticus 16 details the procedures for observance of Yom Kippur in the Tent of Meeting (the portable Temple in the desert), and places a strong emphasis on the special holiness of the location. Later, the Mishnah (Tractate *Yoma*) applies this chapter to the reality of life in Israel, when the Temple was standing in Jerusalem. At that time, the Yom Kippur ritual centered around the entry of the High Priest into the Holy of Holies, the central shrine in the Temple—a once-a-year event of great power. This ritual emphasized the concept that the Holy of Holies was indeed the very center of the world, the *axis mundi,* a unique point at which heaven and earth meet. There are echoes, remnants of this belief in later practice—like the tradition of facing Jerusalem when praying; however, this centrality is no longer very significant in our consciousness, and we tend to assume that we have high-speed wireless access to God wherever we may be in the world.

The traditional Yom Kippur liturgy includes the *Seder Avodah,* a poetic rewriting of the Mishnaic instructions for the sacrificial service of the High Priest on Yom Kippur. It seems to me that this tradition was intended to keep us spatially oriented, to keep the universal messages of the High Holy Days grounded in the message of our rootedness in the Land of Israel. That connection to the land becomes even stronger when we look at some of the details.

In Leviticus 16 we learn that the priest is to set aside two goats—one as a burnt offering and one as the goat for Azazel, the scapegoat. And in verse 21: "Aaron shall lay both his hands upon the head of the live goat and confess over it all the iniquities and transgressions of the Israelites, whatever their sins, putting them on the head of the goat; and it shall be sent off to the wilderness through a designated man . . . and the goat shall be set free in the wilderness." In the Mishnah, (*Yoma,* chapter 6) the procedure is given in more detail: The designated man leads the goat about eight miles out of town, into the Judean desert, to a certain cliff. There is a well-marked route, with ten rest stops, and an entourage to accompany the goat and its chaperone from stop to stop. Then, the two of them walk the last stage alone, and the man pushes the goat off the cliff to oblivion.

The ritual may seem too concrete and thus perhaps too primitive for us. We see our repentance as spiritual, personal, not needing such gross symbolic actions. Yet it is easy to understand why the ritual was so powerful. What I find particularly interesting in it is the route: It is only eight miles from the absolute center of the world to the absolute end of the world—from Somewhere to Nowhere—from the Holy of Holies to the damned, doomed territory of Azazel— from the center of town to the depth of the wilderness. Jerusalem sits on the boundary between Mediterranean climate and desert, between temperate and arid. Perhaps that is part of its secret, its magic, its power in our religious consciousness. It tells us something about ourselves, living on a knife edge, balanced between possibilities, asking ourselves: Where will we be next Yom Kippur?

72. On the Road (*May 19, 2002*)

All distances in the East are measured by hours, not miles. A good horse will walk three miles an hour over nearly any kind of a road; therefore, an hour, here, always stands for three miles. . . . Two hours from Tabor to Nazareth—and as it was an uncommonly narrow, crooked trail, we necessarily met all the camel trains and jackass caravans between Jericho and Jacksonville in that particular place and nowhere else. The donkeys do not matter so much, because they are so small that you can jump your horse over them if he is an animal of spirit, but a camel is not jumpable.

—Mark Twain, *The Innocents Abroad* (1869)

The road leading up to Safed from Karmiel passes through some of the most beautiful scenery in Israel, winding through the mountains of the upper Galilee, past small farming communities, natural woods, and forests planted by the Jewish National Fund. Every switchback reveals a new, breathtaking view. Of course, if you are driving, you can't really enjoy this beauty, as all of your attention is concentrated on staying on the road, wondering if you'll ever get past the double-trailer truck crawling up the mountain ahead of you with a load of rock. (Why are they always trucking rocks around this country? It seems to me that there are plenty wherever you happen to be.) You're also preparing to dodge the idiot coming toward you in your lane in a no-passing zone. It is always a great relief to get to the entrance to town, so that now you can relax and deal with the latest total redesign of traffic patterns in Safed, which seem to have a half-life of about six months.

These days, the adventure of driving to Safed is compounded by a massive road-building project, in which the old, winding, two-lane country road is being replaced by a four-lane highway. And this still being an informal culture, we don't bother with such niceties as giving drivers advance notice of a trench being dug across the highway just around the next curve (just as we can't be bothered with hard hats).

This means that some time (based on the pace, I would say in a couple of years), this adventure will be a nostalgic memory about the good old days of "little Israel," and we will speed smoothly up to Safed in half the time. Except, of course, that this high-speed idyll will come to an abrupt halt at the traffic jam at the entrance to Safed, when all those cars that have been coasting along the four-lane expanse have to squeeze into the overcrowded streets of

Safed, waiting while those who left a few minutes earlier maneuver into all the available spaces left on the sidewalks around the full parking lots.

This phenomenon of improvement of two-lane roads in the periphery into four-lane highways has been in full swing for the past ten years or so, and the results are very impressive. And so are the traffic backups morning and evening and sometimes in between, at every intersection and in every town and city. The squeeze on parking everywhere has given rise to a culture of "just park anywhere"; frustrated with their inability to find a spot, people simply pull their cars onto the sidewalk or the traffic island, or leave them in the passageways of the parking lot. This country is choking in cars, while public transportation languishes.

It is interesting, and sad, to see the dissonance between the environmental reality in Israel today and the utopian vision that motivated many Zionist thinkers. From Theodor Herzl on, there has been a modernist, utopian thread of Zionism that imagined Israel as avoiding all the stupid mistakes of development. Somehow, we would have the wisdom and foresight to take advantage of technology to avoid such ills as pollution, water shortages, consumerism, homelessness, and the like. Alas, it was not to be. Jews may have treasured learning, but when you prick them they still bleed just like anyone else, and when you tempt them, they yield like anyone else—to the lure of the private car, the suburban house, the quality of life that is defined as physical comfort for whoever can afford it. We want the natural beauty of the Galilee, but we want to be able to drive through it quickly, to be able to fence off a piece of it and build our house on it—a house built of cement made from limestone quarried from . . . someone else's backyard.

When we were debating the privatization of the Shorashim *moshav shitufi* (commune), I commented at one meeting that one of the things I most liked about communal living was the sharing of cars, as it seemed to me so ecologically responsible. From the negative response I received it became clear that I was seen as some kind of counterculture nut, and that one of the things that everyone else hated most about communal living was the sharing of cars. This argument makes clear the fundamental conflict between a value system based on the the supremacy of the individual and one based on the primacy of the needs of the group. While it seems to me clear that the sustainability of Israel depends on building trains instead of highways, cities instead of sprawling suburbs, it is also clear that there are very powerful social and psychological forces working against that vision. Perhaps we need a Jeremiah or an Amos to remind us, as they did almost three millennia ago, that we Jews are supposed to place vision above personal interests, that our collective future depends on our individual behavior. But then, did anyone listen to them then? Would anyone hear them now?

73. Wheels *(November 28, 2004)*

They [Joseph's brothers] sat down to eat, when they looked up and saw a caravan of Ishmaelites traveling from Gilead. Their camels were loaded with ladanum, balm, and mastic; they were heading down to Egypt.

—Genesis 37:25

Since the most ancient times, caravan routes have crossed through *Eretz Israel,* connecting the lands east of the Jordan Valley with Egypt and Africa beyond. Spices and textiles, jewels and salt and minerals have been carried back and forth along the routes that run up the coast, through the east-west valleys, and up and down the Jordan rift valley. And, often, armies have followed the same routes, as this land was the meeting—and confrontation—place between East and West.

From the early twentieth century until 1948, these same routes were plied by railroads. You could get on a train in Haifa and travel to Cairo, to Beirut, to Damascus, and even to Mecca. Palestine was a hub for the whole Middle East; first the Turks and later the British invested heavily in the development of rail transport—for goods, for pilgrims to Mecca, for armies. Those days are almost forgotten today. You can walk along the track toward Beirut at Rosh Hanikra, right up to the cement wall that blocks it at the Lebanese border. I remember, in the late '60s, traveling in the newly conquered West Bank, seeing the remnants of the tracks that had led eastward, before they were ripped up for scrap. You can still visit the shells of train stations in towns that haven't seen a train in over fifty years (for example, in Afula and Bet Shean).

Today, Israelis tend to see ourselves as an island, as if we had no land connection—our "nearest neighbors" are in Europe, to which our only connection is via Ben Gurion Airport. This perception is, by the way, obsolete to some extent; you can drive to Egypt, and many Israelis do, to vacation in Sinai and beyond, even in these years of "cold peace." And there are all kinds of traffic over the bridges to Jordan: tourists, merchants, pilgrims to Mecca—and Israeli Arabs studying at Jordanian universities, coming home for the weekend. When the peace treaty was signed with Jordan and the "new Middle East" seemed to be dawning, the tabloid papers ran front-page maps showing the driving times to various destinations in Europe via Syria and Turkey. That enthusiastic optimism has dimmed, but the fact is that we are no longer the island we once were. However, for now, the rails still stop at the borders.

For years, the trains in Israel were quaint, inconvenient, uncomfortable, infrequent, and not taken very seriously. The passengers were mostly soldiers, who rode for free. But in the past ten years or so, there has been a quantum leap, as huge investments have been made in rail travel. New trains, new stations, new routes, a new mentality, have made the trains a showplace of what we can do. They are packed with commuters and students and families on outings. A few weeks ago, the new terminal at Ben Gurion Airport opened—a massive structure meant to put Israel on a par with European destinations. And the terminal is served by a rail line that connects hourly to the main line between Nahariya and Beersheba. I suppose, in a sense, that what this means is that you can get on a train in Nahariya and get off in London or New York. The seamlessness of the connection reduces our isolation by one more degree. However, it's still not the real thing, and I continue to wait for the day — which I believe will come — when we'll board the train in Karmiel and transfer in Istanbul for the Orient Express to Paris.

74. Country Mouse *(April 23, 2006)*

Over the years, my family has lived in Beersheba (one year), Jerusalem (five years), and in the Galilee at Shorashim (sixteen years). From each of those vantage points, Tel Aviv was far off and nasty: Secular, urban, Western, polluted, crowded — why would you want to go there unless you had to? OK, so it had a beach. But to the visitor from the periphery (or from Holy Jerusalem), the face of Tel Aviv was the old central bus station, hot and filthy, where pedestrians and buses dodged each other between stands piled high with pirated music and fake designer clothes, and you didn't have to ask where the restrooms were — you could just follow the scent of stale urine. This was the first modern Jewish city, the cultural capital of the Jewish state?

Tel Aviv, actually the name of a community of exiles in Babylonia (Ezekiel 3:15), was named for the translation of Herzl's 1902 utopian novel *Oldnewland*: a *tel* is an ancient ruin, an archaeological mound, and *aviv* means "spring" (the season). The pioneers who bought lots in the sand dunes in 1909 saw themselves as the creators of a renewed Jewish culture.

> So [Judaism] seeks to return to its historic centre, in order to live there a life of natural development, to bring its

powers into play in every department of human culture, to develop and perfect those national possessions which it has acquired up to now, and thus to contribute to the common stock of humanity, in the future as in the past, a great national culture, the fruit of the unhampered activity of a people living according to its own spirit. (Ahad Ha'am, *Jewish State and Jewish Problem* [1897])

But to my judgmental eye, Tel Aviv was all new with no roots, all a daunting synthesis of global and Middle Eastern pop culture, built on sand dunes.

Today there is a new bus station, which is actually not much different from the old one except that the buses are kept away from the pedestrians, and there is air-conditioning. The shady merchants and the smelly bathrooms have been lovingly preserved. Meanwhile, the old bus station, which was actually a tangle of streets and alleys, has become a community of thousands of foreign workers, legal and illegal; a polyglot, multicultural neighborhood where poor migrant workers, idealistic social workers, and tough-guy immigration cops all dodge the Palestinian suicide bombers who seem to be drawn to the area.

As the years have gone by, however, it seems that my aversion to Tel Aviv has mellowed. Maybe it's the prolonged quiet of life on the periphery; maybe it's a more mature understanding of the nature of culture—and Jewish culture, in particular. Whatever it is, when planning a recent two-day getaway, we decided to depart from our usual custom of seeking a bed-and-breakfast in a "natural" setting, like the Golan or the Negev, and book a room in the heart of Tel Aviv.

And guess what? It turns out that "secular, urban, Western, crowded, polluted" can be seen as vibrant, open, multicultural, and humming with life. Rich museums of art and archaeology, hundreds of cafés, interesting restaurants (even kosher), that magnificent beach, crowded open-air markets piled with tempting produce and colorful textiles, graceful Bauhaus buildings on broad avenues, and old stone houses on narrow alleys. Strip shows and synagogues, uncrossable streets and green parks, slums and mansions. A real city, with all the ills and beauties that are inherent in large modern cities. I think Ahad Ha'am, critical as he often was, would be impressed with the culture that Tel Aviv embodies and exudes. Western as it is, it is in Hebrew. And the drama and literature and art and music that flourish in it do indeed draw from the Jewish experience, refracting it through a modern or postmodern lens. Which is, I suppose, what this whole exercise is all about.

75. *Chamsin* (September 24, 2006)

The Lord God provided a gourd, which grew up over Jonah, to provide shade for his head and save him from discomfort. Jonah was very happy about the plant. But the next day at dawn God provided a worm, which attacked the plant so that it withered. And when the sun rose, God provided an . . . east wind; the sun beat down on Jonah's head and he became faint. He begged for death, saying, "I would rather die than live."

—Jonah 4:6–8

The book of Jonah is traditionally read as the haftarah on Yom Kippur afternoon, and it seems pretty clear that the reason has to do with the book's message that God wants our repentance, not our suffering. Indeed, if even the cows of Nineveh can repent and be forgiven (see 3:8), so can we. However, perhaps there is another, seasonal, connection between the day and the book that we shouldn't overlook. To teach Jonah the lesson of God's desire to preserve the lives of all of God's creatures, God causes him to experience the death of the plant that has been shading him on a hot day: If you, God suggests, are so upset about the death of a lowly vine, then how should I not be upset by the prospect of the destruction of a great city?! Notice the interesting detail: When the gourd withers, Jonah is blasted by a hot east wind—and is so uncomfortable that he wishes he were dead.

Apparently, the author was familiar with the dreaded *chamsin* (in Egyptian Arabic and Hebrew slang), *sharav* (in formal Hebrew), or *sirocco* (in southern Europe—see *Death in Venice* by Thomas Mann), the hot, dry, wind blowing in from the Arabian desert, that dries the throat, coats everything with fine dust, shortens the temper, and causes headaches in epidemic proportions.

The heat and dust sap your energy; it is hard to develop the ambition to do much of anything. If you close all the windows, the house becomes like an oven. If you open them, it becomes like a turbo oven. Unfortunately, the turbo effect works outdoors as well, and *chamsin* season is forest fire and brush fire season; often there is smoke mixed with the dust, as the wind whips the flames—and carries the smoke with it. While not scientifically supported, it is easy to believe, on a severe *chamsin* day, that the tinder-dry thistles along the roadside could burst into flames spontaneously.

Often, a *chamsin* ends suddenly, with a temperature drop of twenty degrees in an hour or so, and with a brief shower—large, warm drops, which, cleaning the dust out of the air as they fall, land as splashes of mud, which soon dries, leaving windows and cars with a blotchy light brown coating.

This weather phenomenon, which generally lasts from a few days to a week, is characteristic of spring and fall in these parts; indeed, a common topic of small talk during the ten days of penitence are the chances that a *chamsin* will strike on Yom Kippur, making the day one of significantly greater misery for thousands of people. The heat and dryness permeate everything—shade doesn't help much, and it is all too easy to suffer from dehydration before you know what hit you—not a good situation for a fast day. And if a *chamsin* strikes during Sukkot, you can sit in your sukkah and listen to the green leaves you spread on the roof drying and shriveling in real time.

This year, there were some days of *chamsin* before Yom Kippur, but the holiday itself was quite moderate: hot but not really unpleasant. We knew from experience what Jonah felt, but fortunately we didn't have to go through it ourselves this time. So we were free to laugh, with God, at the prophet who had no sense of humor, and to look forward to the cooler, more forgiving days that we knew will soon be upon us.

76. Mitzpeh Ramon *(August 12, 2007)*

I accounted to your favor the devotion of your youth,
Your love as a bride—
How you followed Me in the desert,
In a land not sown.

—Jeremiah 2:2

When the St. Louis Arches youth circus joined the Galilee Circus (a Jewish-Arab youth circus) for a performance tour of the country, the group spent an afternoon touring the old city of Jerusalem, viewing the grandiose mosques on the Temple Mount, and visiting the Western Wall and the Church of the Holy Sepulchre. Over the centuries, Jews, Muslims, and Christians have invested untold amounts of wealth—and blood—in conquering, controlling, beautifying, and fortifying their particular bits of real estate in Jerusalem. Of course, this is not just any real estate, but holy ground, the place in which God's presence is believed to dwell. And for many, this indwelling is almost palpable. Even among the kids in our group, ordinary middle-class teenagers living in secular environments, visiting these holy sites had an impact: a Muslim girl spoke with reverence of her experiences of praying at the Al-Aqsa Mosque; there were American Christian kids who were truly moved by the experience of touching the Stone of Unction, where Jesus's body is believed to have been anointed prior to burial; and for many of the Jews, visiting the Wall at night had its own spiritual impact. Even so, sometimes I wonder if God realized that getting involved in the residential property market would cause us all so much grief.

This question was cast in sharp relief the next day, when we drove from Jerusalem to Mitzpeh Ramon, in the heart of the Negev. We left late in the afternoon, and didn't arrive until late at night. Our accommodations were at a fairly primitive imitation-Bedouin-style campsite, whose most noteworthy characteristic at the time of our arrival was the lack of electricity. It took us a while to get settled and prepare dinner in almost total darkness (near the beginning of the month, there wasn't even moonlight). But then we realized that out in the desert, without electric lights, you can see things that you can't see at home: mostly, the Milky Way in all its majesty. And when the sun rises over the mountains in the morning, there you are, exposed, vulnerable, squeezing into whatever shade you can find. Or looking out across the spectacular scenery of the Ramon Crater, feeling small.

The contrast between the crowded holy sites of Jerusalem—protected by X-ray machines and metal detectors, built, decorated, and controlled by people—and the silent, lonely majesty of the desert, which seems to overpower human attempts to control it, was striking. Especially when you remember that Moses (who, of course, never set foot in Jerusalem) had his conversations with God in the desert (as did Elijah, after him); that Jesus spent a pivotal forty days and nights there (Matthew 4:1–4); and that Muhammad's entire biography is rooted in the desert. While the Children of Israel wandered for forty years in the desert as a punishment and a purification after the demonstration of faithlessness by the spies (Numbers 14:26–35), the memory morphed over time into a positive one: Note, in the text above, that Jeremiah refers to the desert years as the honeymoon in God's relationship to Israel. It seems we have always had an ambivalent relationship with this region. The vulnerability and smallness we feel here makes us more dependent on God—but that, apparently, is not always such a good feeling. It is easier and more comforting to communicate with God by inserting a note between the stones of the Western Wall than it is to stand speechless and all alone in the middle of nowhere. Moreover, the Western Wall we can own, while the desert makes our concepts of possession and control feel a bit ridiculous.

God's presence may be in residence in the sacred edifices of Jerusalem, but I have no doubt God has a time-share in Mitzpeh Ramon.

Permissions and Sources

All quotes from the Torah come from *The Torah: A Modern Commentary*, revised edition, edited by W. Gunther Plaut (URJ Press, 2005). All quotes from Prophets and Writings come from *The Tanakh: A New Translation of* THE HOLY SCRIPTURES © 1985 by The Jewish Publication Society. Used with permission.

Unless otherwise noted, all translations from Hebrew are the author's.

Sources of quoted material:

Pg. 28, 192: Mark Twain, *Innocents Abroad* © 1869; pg. 28: Rabbi Nachman of Bratslav Rambam (Maimonides); pg. 38: *Guide for the Perplexed* 3:43; pg. 40: *Mishnah Avodah Zarah* 3:4; pg. 57: Babylonian Talmud, *Sanhedrin* 17b; pg 62: *Pirkei Avot* 1:14; pg. 65: Rambam (Maimonides), *Mishneh Torah,* Gifts to the Poor 7:10, *Mishneh Torah,* Mourning 14:3; pg. 67: Wisdom of Ben Sira 11:29; pg. 72: *Pirkei D'Rabbi Eliezer* 24; pg. 77: Jacob Klatzkin, *Boundaries* © 1914; pg. 85: Shlomo Schiller, *Zionism and*

Religion; pg. 89: *Mishnah Hagigah* 1:8; pg. 90: Achad Ha'am, *Shabbat and Zionism*; pg. 99: Rambam (Maimonides), *Mishneh Torah*, Laws Regarding Pagans 10:5; pg. 107: Israel Declaration of Independence; pg. 118: Anton Shamas, "At Half-Mast—Myths, Symbols, and Rituals of the Emerging State: A Personal Testimony of an Israeli Arab," in *New Perspectives on Israeli History*, ed. L. Silberstein © 1991; pg. 126: Qur'an, Sura 37; pg. 139: Talmud, *Sanhedrin* 70b; pg. 142-3: *Sifrei D'varim, Ha'azinu* 316; pg. 147: Babylonian Talmud, *Shabbat* 21b; pg. 148: Midrash *Mechilta D'Rabbi Shimon bar Yochai* 13; pg. 162: Dr. Max Nordau's keynote address at the Second Zionist Congress, 1898; pg. 197: Ahad Ha'am, *Jewish State and Jewish Problem (1897)*.

The author and publisher gratefully acknowledge the following for permission to reprint previously published works:

CENTRAL CONFERENCE OF AMERICAN RABBIS: Excerpts from *Gates of Repentance* © 1978. Used by permission of the Central Conference of American Rabbis, all rights reserved. (pg. 35)

UZI CHITMAN (HITMAN): Lyrics from "Kan" written by Uzi Chitman, performed by Orna and Moshe Datz on their CD "The Best of Duo Datz" © 1994. Used by permission of ACUM. (pg. 21)

JEWISH PUBLICATION SOCIETY: Excerpts reprinted from *Morning Stars*, © 1967 by Zalman Shazar, published by The Jewish Publication Society, with the permission of the publisher. (pg. 168–9)

JONI MITCHELL: Lyrics from "The Circle Game" written by Joni Mitchell from *Ladies of the Canyon* © 1970. Used by permission from Alfred Publishing Co., Inc. (pg. 33)

PENGUIN GROUP: Excerpts from *To Jerusalem and Back: A Personal Account* © 1976 by Saul Bellow. Used by permission of Viking Penguin, a division of Penguin Putnam, Inc. (pg. 159-60)

RANDOM HOUSE, INC.: Excerpts from *Exodus* © 1958 by Leon Uris. Used by permission of Bantam Books, an imprint of Random House, Inc. (pg. 150)

NAOMI SHEMER: Lyrics from "Al Kol Eleh (For All These Things)" written by Naomi Shemer from *Al Hadvash Ve'al Ha'oketz* © 1981. Used by permission of NMC United Entertainment Ltd. (pg. 171)